The Process of Play Directing

FROM CONCEPT TO CURTAIN

Bob May

Skye Bridge Publishing
Asheville, NC

Copyright © 2016 Bob May

All rights reserved. No part of this publication may be reproduced, distributed, or transmitted in any form or by any means, including photocopying, recording, or other electronic or mechanical methods, without the prior written permission of the publisher, except in the case of brief quotations embodied in critical reviews and certain other noncommercial uses permitted by copyright law. For permission requests, please contact the author directly.

Edited by D. A. Sarac
theeditingpen.com

Cover Design by Gustav Carlson
touristunknown.com

Skye Bridge Publishing
Asheville, NC
Please contact
Publisher@SkyeBridgePublishing.com

Printed in the United States of America

The Process of Play Directing / Bob May —1st ed.
ISBN 978-0-9967583-3-8

Contents

Foreword vii
Introduction xi

CHAPTER 1
Defining the Director 1

CHAPTER 2
Prerehearsal Work 5

CHAPTER 3
Rehearsal 55

CHAPTER 4
Tips 79

About the Author 102
Show Credits 106
List of Authors Whose Plays Appear in Photographs and Figures 109

PRAISE FOR THE PROCESS OF PLAY DIRECTING:

FROM CONCEPT TO CURTAIN

"I liked your book a lot. Any director could learn a lot from it. Good work! I think the simplicity, and right to the point nature of your writing enhances it."
Karen Owings, Musical Director, Little Rock, AR

"I love how short and direct the chapters are. As always, your writing is clear and concise. I truly feel as though you're talking to me. The thank-you section underscores what you do so well as a director and what is different about what you do than what most other directors do, and that's express gratitude and reinforce that theatre is a collaborative medium. That's one of the great lessons I learned from you that I took into my career as a director, and it's honestly some of the best feedback I got from actors. And I think actors appreciate it because it's rare."
Cristopher Tibbetts, Director, Minneapolis, MN

ACKNOWLEDGMENTS

I directed my first show in 1970, and I always learn something every time I do a show even after all the productions I've brought to life. I would like to thank all the hundreds (if not thousands) of actors, choreographers, musical directors, designers, technicians, and producers I've worked with over the years, including Steve Antenucci, Peta Barrett, Amy Borash, Chad Bradford, Lee Christiansen, Matt Cooper, Jerry L. Crawford, Bob Dryden, R. Watson Dreissig, James Erdahl, Larry Gochberg, Jan Hilton, Jeff Koep, Dwight Larson, Ed Marek, Davey Marlin-Jones, Joe Meils, Jacqueline Mudge, Lauren Nickisch, Karen Owings, Erik (EP) Paulson, Bob Platte, Frank Rogers, Sharon Selberg, Brian C. Smith, Jeff Stroman, Don Sunquist, Nikki Webster, and Terry Wright.

There are a few people that are distinct as they really taught me very special lessons. They are Dick Cermele, Joy Breckenridge, Kari Anderson, Lynn Musgrave, and Cris Tibbetts.

To my wife, Cathy.

Foreword

It is with great pleasure and pride that I write this foreword for Bob. More than twenty years ago, I had the privilege of not only working as an actor in several of Bob's productions, but I also was able to take his directing class. In my time onstage under Bob's direction, I grew exponentially as an actress. Bob is the consummate professional and knows instinctively how to bring out not only the best performance in every actor, but also how to help them understand the workings of the "machine" that is the play itself.

Over the course of the past twenty years, I have worked professionally with many directors but none who were able to articulate as clearly the process of putting together a seamless production. In addition to being the best director I have ever had the pleasure of working with, Bob was undoubtedly one of the best teachers I have ever encountered. His directing class, in particular, was tough. Very tough. He required his students to dissect the play to the smallest detail, to consider every aspect of every show we were part of. In effect, he taught his students to become "microsurgeons of the theater"—to take apart every play and then put it back together and make it work better. He taught us to create a textbook of sorts. This "prompt book" was our final exam. Through his guidance, we were able to put together a fully prepared director's plan for the show of our choosing. This plan included not just the blocking of the show but rehearsal schedule, imagery, set design, costume designs, actor intent and objectives for every scene (sometimes every line!), preshow preparations, prop lists, and a complete breakdown of the show's "heartbeat" or pulse. We were required to know our show backward and forward, to document each movement and moment of how we wanted our show to evolve and come to life. It was grueling. It took weeks to prepare. It was also the best theatrical class I have ever had. I had no real idea at the time (I was all of twenty years old) just how important this class would be or how much of a mark it would leave on my life in theater from then on.

Fast-forward twenty-seven years. I am now forty-seven years old. My plans to act for a living eventually gave way to being a mom and having a family, but theater is still consistently a huge part of my life. I regularly choreograph and direct productions in the community in which I live. Although I have a system or routine that I follow for every show I direct or choreograph, I am always anxious to learn more or to observe another person's process, so I was thrilled when Bob sent me a copy of his directing book. What could be better than a little "brush up" on his wisdom? What was truly amazing to me when I read it, is how much of "my process" was actually his process. As I matured moved farther away from my college years, I had begun to forget where my knowledge had come from, assuming as most people would, that I learned things on my own through trial and error. Imagine my (pleasant) surprise when I realized that these skills, rules, and ideas had not only been taught to me by a trusted mentor, but that they had stayed with me over the course of years' worth of theatrical productions. The lessons he taught me so many years ago both onstage and in the classroom still resonate within me... more than I had ever imagined. During my experiences as a director (and actor), I have often had "his voice" in my head reminding me of certain aspects of a performance. "No straight lines!" or "Smile, this isn't *Death of a Salesman*, we're doing a MUSICAL" are direct Bob quotes that I still say to this day, but so many subtle choices I make as a director/actor also come from him. Things like choosing appropriate preshow music, intermission music, how to give notes to your performers, and how to schedule rehearsals are a few great examples. I had not realized until reading this book that I mirrored Bob's process almost exactly for every show I direct.

When I am onstage, I am always acutely aware of how to create a picture when I interact with other performers—how to avoid upstaging others or myself through movement, how to use my levels. None of these habits were ones I had directly attributed to Bob until I read this book. I think the mark of any good teacher is the ability not to just provide information, but to teach it... There is a difference. When you teach your students, the information you present becomes part of them. The knowledge is absorbed and applied repeatedly over the course of their lives. It changes who they are.

It is rare to find a teacher who can accomplish this. Bob is one of those teachers. His gift of direction stays with you. It becomes part of who you are both as a performer and a director. I am forever grateful for the time I spent learning from him, and I am equally grateful that he has finally put his wisdom down on paper so that I can continually refer to it for guidance. I cannot recommend this book highly enough. It should be in every theater classroom, in every student backpack, and on the shelf of every performer/director. Its quick, no-nonsense, succinct format makes it ideal for actors and would-be directors everywhere!

Amy Borash
Choreographer, Dance Instructor, Actor, Director
Baxter, MN

Introduction

What is *The Process of Play Directing?* It is a brief but to-the-point approach to the art of directing. It's a checklist for the seasoned director and a quick how-to for the novice director who wants to learn some of the tricks of the trade. More importantly, it's a reflection of my thoughts on directing compiled in concept-to-curtain order.

So who am I to be writing a book on directing (I've never directed on Broadway or a major motion picture), and why would you want to read a book on directing that I have written? Because I've survived and made a living as a working director in this screwy business we call show business. I was encouraged by my many collaborators over the years to write this book. I've suffered for my art. I've eaten many a cold cheeseburger at a heated tech rehearsal. I've neglected relationships for the sake of the show. The theatre fuels my blood type: A-positive for the show!

I've been in the theatre trenches for fifty years and guided over four hundred and fifty shows to opening night at professional, dinner, community, high school, and university theatres all over the world.

This book is not going to make you a great director. It's not going to guarantee that after reading it you'll direct on Broadway and win a Tony award. It is going to help you be a better director by understanding the basic tools of the trade learned through my many years at the helm.

Directing is an art. It is not just coaching actors on their performances. That's part of it, but there is so much more to the art of directing. Why is directing an art? On any stage, but especially a proscenium stage, a director paints a picture just as a painter does on a canvas or a photographer does with film.

And just as a head football coach maps out plays for the players and team to win, a director manipulates his performers in the same winning process. The director's most important job is to interpret the playwright's words.

I have always prided myself that I was trained as a director; I was not just an actor who wanted to direct. If you are the actor who wants to direct or finds himself in the position of directing, I hope this book will help. If you're a seasoned director, it will remind you of old and hopefully new techniques to use.

The book is divided into four sections: Defining the Director, Prerehearsal Work, Rehearsal, and Tips. So why don't I stop talking about what I did and get to it?

—Bob May

CHAPTER 1

Defining the Director

The Feather Theory

The theatre is a collaborative art. It is also a business full of egos, and I don't mean that in a negative way. You must have an ego to even want to be in this business, much less survive in it. There is a pecking order of power for all those egotistical artists gathered in one common place, the theatre.

My feather theory puts that pecking order into a simple logic. This theory is not meant to anger any culture. It is out of respect that I came up with this theory. Cowboy and Indian flicks and TV shows about the Wild West dominated my youth. Warner Bros. TV had many popular westerns including *Sugarfoot, Cheyenne, Maverick,* and *The Rifleman* that I watched religiously.

So what is the feather theory? It's very simple. Just as the chief of an Indian tribe has the most feathers in his headdress and is the leader with the most power, it is the same in the theatre. Producers have four feathers, directors have three, designers have two, and actors have one.

An intelligent producer will sit on his four feathers and let the director that he hired do his/her job. The director with the three feathers is next in command and has the final say in all artistic decisions. (The producer/director relationship could be an entire book, and it will be dealt with briefly in the next section.)

Having the most power doesn't mean that you stop listening to any suggestions that the collaborators with fewer feathers have. A smart director learns how to filter through the fodder the fellow feather holders feed him.

Never say "no" to any suggestion. Just remember how many feathers are in your headdress and wear them intelligently.

Bob May and the cast of *City Lights*

If You Want to Do a Solo Act, Get into Photography

I promised myself after graduating from undergraduate school with a Bachelor of Arts degree in theatre (the emphasis was in directing) that I would only work in the theatre to make my living. That was a tough promise to keep. Although I only wanted to direct, I found myself building sets, gathering props, making costumes, and even acting to make that living in the theatre. And when I got a directing job, I would sometimes find myself doing all those other jobs too, but only being paid to direct.

I felt like I was doing a solo act at the circus without a net. But that is not the solo act I am talking about. That does happen with some directing gigs, but that is not the preferred method of directing. As I said in the feather theory section, the theatre is a collaborative art. It's the many minds working on the same piece of art that excited me. I developed some very strong bonds with designers from all of the disciplines that have lasted for years.

A very good friend developed into a fine set designer. Unfortunately for the theatre world, she eventually left the theatre because she did not like the collaborative process. Having directors (me and others) ask for changes with her set designs was not her idea of art. She went on to get a BFA in photography. She laughs now and says, "In the dark room, the negative never talks back to me or tells me how to do things." She is in complete control. She is a singular artist, and enjoys a successful solo act.

You cannot be a solo artist in the theatre. Remember, the theatre is a collaborative art. That's what I love about it. A pride of people all working on the same project to produce the best product they can to please the paying patrons of the play.

So if you want to do a solo act… get into photography. And be the person taking the photo of me during my time in graduate school in Las Vegas.

City Lights (Las Vegas, NV)

The Only God in the Theatre Is Dionysus

A director is nothing without a team of good designers and talented actors supporting a vision. Get over the notion that you are God. If you have that attitude, your designers or actors won't give their all to the project.

Good designers will trust your concept, and actors will accept your guidance if they respect you. In the end, that will help you fulfill your vision and make the show a success.

Dionysus is the only God needed in the theatre.

CHAPTER 2

Prerehearsal Work

Read and Reread

Once you know what show you're directing, read the script and then reread the script. And then reread it again. Then read it without reading the stage directions. Just read the dialogue. Does the show still make sense?

In a play, if something is not in the dialogue, it won't be clear to the audience. Plays are not films. In a film, the camera can zoom in on a clock to let the audience know what time it is. In a play, a character must say what time it is. Keep reading. Know it backward and forward. Read it so much that when you're not reading it, you're still thinking about it. Let the show become part of you and you part of the show.

The New York Theatre Critics' Reviews

Do your homework. Read up on the show you're directing. Most of the time you will be directing a show that was originally produced on Broadway, and the reviews of that show will help you gain insights you might not have thought about and give you a better understanding of the show.

In the resource section of any major library, there is a wonderful collection of books called The New York Theatre Critics Reviews. This resource gem contains all the reviews of every show that opened on or off Broadway. It is bound by year. Check the opening date of the play you're directing in the front of the script to find what year you need to reference.

For a fee, there is a company called Package Publicity Service, Inc. that will send you copies of all the reviews. The contact information is:

Package Publicity Service Inc.
255 W 88th Street
Apt 3e
New York, NY 10024-1717
(212) 255-2872

Conceptualize Your Baby

The Fantasticks
(Jones and Schmidt)

After all the reading, rereading, and research, it's time to decide what you want to say with the show—your baby. Some directors call it their commanding image or their metaphor. I like the word concept.

When I directed *The Fantasticks*, I thought the plot of boy meets girl, boy loses girl, and boy gets girl back was so simple. I don't mean that in a bad way. The show works wonderfully. So with this simple story came thoughts of "good/bad," "right/wrong," or just "night/day." From that, my concept became "black or white." And that's what became the show's metaphor—black or white.

The sets and costumes were all done in black and white. It's amazing how patterns in the material used for costumes can create the illusion of color. I wanted to convey the innocence of the characters and show, and I thought the black-and-white concept illustrated that. And then at the end of the show when the characters in the play lose their innocence, color was introduced in the sets and costumes.

The play, *Winterset*, by Maxwell Anderson, is about a young man who enjoys his freedom but finds himself in love with a young girl from NYC and caught in the city.

The commanding image related to the designers was a prison. The set designer made the buildings of New

York feel like prison bars holding the young couple in the city. The costumes subtlety suggested prison dress, and the lighting was oppressive.

When I directed *Agnes of God* by John Pielmeier, for the set design I asked for three round platforms made simply of unvarnished wood. They were meant to represent the three faces of Catholicism: the Father, Son, and Holy Ghost. The interconnected circles represented each of the three characters in the show, their circle of life and how their lives connected or intersected with each other. I wanted the plain, unvarnished wood to represent the cross that Jesus was nailed to.

A concept doesn't have to be complicated. It can be as simple as just telling the story the playwright intended. Don't let concept get in your way of telling the story.

Designers Are Your Friends, So Trust Them

At the first production meeting with the design staff, share your concept with your designers. After explaining it to them, give them a week or so to think about what you've shared.

Meet again and listen to how they are going to support your concept. Talk, discuss, and enjoy the creative process.

Remember: The designers are on your side. They are your creative partners, your friends. Listen to them; they can help your concept develop and come alive.

Have Weekly Production Meetings

Meet with your designers. Meet with them often before rehearsal begins and especially once rehearsal is in progress. Weekly production meetings keep everyone on the same page.

Have you added a prop or cut a costume? With weekly production meetings, no one is ever surprised when things change. And believe me, things will change.

I directed a production of *Chicago* that was voted one of the top ten shows of the year by the Minneapolis *StarTribune*. My concept of the show was a reflection of the press making heroes out of murderers. The set designer said to me, "Only in America." And that became the bigger metaphor and was illustrated wonderfully in the last song when we flew in an American flag that filled the entire stage behind Roxie and Velma as they danced to "The Hot Honey Rag."

Chicago (Kander and Ebb)

I wrote and directed *Beanie and the Bamboozling Book Machine* in 1989. It's a fantasy-adventure about a kid science wiz who invents a bookreading machine to read for him, and while demonstrating the machine, the witches from *The Wizard of Oz*, *Snow White*, and *Hansel and Gretel* escape from their books. Professor

Librum and his Decimals from Bookworld help restore order and get the witches back into their books.

I directed the show once again in 2004, and the costume designer opened my eyes to what could be done with this fantasy. She suggested we put the Decimals on roller skates, and it added a wonderful spectacle to the show. I now only see the Decimals on roller skates.

Beanie and the Bamboozling Book Machine
(May, Tibbetts, Booth)

Fiddler on the Roof is usually designed in dark colors to reflect the earth tones and repression of the poor Russian Jews in their shtetls, pre-World War II. As I

Fiddler on the Roof (Bock, Harnick, Stein)

read the script, I saw it as a celebration of life and a survival of a culture. The title of the show was based on a painting by Chagall, and after looking at that painting and other Chagall paintings, I realized the concept of the show must be based on the bright colors found in Chagall's work.

Instead of using earth tones and dark colors in the sets and costumes, we used the bright colors of the rainbow. The sets also reflected the abstract qualities of the paintings of Chagall. The costumes brought smiles to the audience's faces with their happy colors. The bright production brought new meaning to the show.

When I directed *A Shot in the Dark* by Marcel Achard, my concept was a shooting target. Most of the action takes place in a courtroom, and I wanted the witness chair in the center of the target, in the bull's-eye. The

A Shot in the Dark (Achard)

set designer did a wonderful job creating this illusion.

The concept for the Feydeau farce *A Flea in Her Ear* was a puzzle. The show is like a big puzzle as all the characters try to figure out what is going on.

A Flea in Her Ear (Feydeau)

The lighting designer adds so much to a show's concept. And the lighting pulls the set and costumes together. So many moods can be set with the lighting.

Lighting: *The Fantasticks* (Jones and Schmidt)

There is nothing wrong with bonding with the designers that you work well with. During my many years freelancing in Minneapolis, I found that I preferred working with certain designers over ones I had not worked with.

We helped each other look good. After working together on so many shows, we knew what we liked, developed a shorthand method of communication, and complimented each other.

Don't Forget Sound

I've spent a lot of time talking about the scenic, costume, and lighting designers, but don't forget about the sound designers. That not only includes sound effects that are in the show, like a phone ringing or a gunshot, but also music at various parts of the production that supports your concept.

I always have music playing in the house (preshow music) from the moment the audience starts to enter until the show begins. That usually lasts for a half an hour. The music should set mood for the show the audience is about to see. For the show *Boys in the Band*, I played overtures from various musicals. Love songs were played prior to my production of *Children of a Lessor God*.

Open each act with music that supports your concept or the theme of the show. The opening of a light comedy would have up-tempo, light music to introduce the show. *Dracula* would have something spooky or mysterious. Make sure you fade the preshow music, then fade your house lights while beginning your opening music. Then fade the preset lighting. Let your opening of show music establish for a bit in the black and then fade the stage lights up as you fade out the opening music.

Make sure you bridge all scenes and cover all scene changes with music. Have special music to accompany the ending of scenes and acts. Play music throughout all intermissions and during the curtain call. Also play music as the audience exits the theatre.

But I Am a One-Person Show

Many directors in educational theatre don't have the luxury of having a support design team and have to do it all as a one-person show. Been there, done that! Just remember that your set, costume, and light design should support your directorial concept.

And then enlist the help of the actors in the show, students interested in helping with the show, and parents of those students to help build the set, sew the costumes, hang the lights, record the sound, and gather the props.

The theatre is a collaborative art. Your support staff is just made up of volunteers who will be looking for you to guide them in all areas. I have found that many students interested in theatre have parents who are also interested in theatre. A father who is an electrician can help with the lights. Or a parent in construction knows how to build sets.

Someone in radio or television can do sound, others can help with costumes. Divide the props that are needed for the show among the actors in the show. That way one person is not getting them all.

Don't forget press releases and promo photos.

Make sure that you recognize everyone that helped when the show closes; maybe an awards ceremony or just a closing banquet or party. At least say thank you after each building or sewing session.

Choreographers and Music Directors

When doing a musical, choreographers and music directors should be included in all the prerehearsal and weekly production meetings. When it comes to feathers, those two positions almost wear as many as the director; they have two and a half feathers. It's important that both of them are very familiar with your concept and agree with it. Their creativity is a reflection of you, and you have to trust their expertise.

I have choreographed musicals that I have directed, but I am not a dancer. Finding the right choreographer is so important. I always talk through each musical number with the choreographer conceptually. And just like designers, the choreographer's input is always welcome, and ultimately his or her creations are a reflection of your concept.

I've been blessed with working with several choreographers that helped make my productions so much better.

It's the same thing with music directors. Make sure the lines of communication are open with this vital part of a musical; be on the same page with each song and dance number.

Being a fan of Stephen Sondheim, and having taught an honors college class for many years on the genius composer, and having directed several of his shows, I learned through his work that each song should be looked at like it were a mini one-act play. Sondheim has stated that his mentor, Oscar Hammerstein, taught him this theory.

The musical *Chicago* (Kander and Ebb)

This lesson has helped me with the success of musicals, and it is illustrated wonderfully by Bernadette Peters in her solo concerts. I was lucky enough to see Ms. Peters in Las Vegas, and each of her songs were sung, staged, and choreographed as though they were a short one-act play. She has a DVD titled *In Concert*, or you can watch her in two Sondheim musicals that are on DVD, *Into the Woods* and *Sunday in the Park with George* for wonderful examples of this theory.

Understanding the Show

Plays are man-made. They are not real life. Real life doesn't happen or unfold as neatly structured as plays do. Just look at the spelling of the word playwright. It's WRIGHT, not WRITE.

And why is that?

Because all plays are crafted. Just as a shipwright makes a ship, or a wheelwright makes a wheel, a playwright makes a play. Plays are not real life. There are rules to follow if the playwright is going to have a structurally sound play. And as directors, you must understand these rules so you can dissect and interpret the play—find out what makes it tick.

To really understand the show, you must dissect the script as thoroughly as a coroner does to comprehend why a corpse stopped ticking, but in your case you want to know what makes the script tick. Good play analysis is the key to the directing process. There are four elements to understanding the show. They are:

1). Character objectives
2). Dramatic action
3). PASTO
4). Units

Character Objectives

There are two kinds of character objectives: superobjectives and unit-by-unit objectives.

All characters want something (objective). And they try to fulfill that something like it were a desperate quest. That quest is the superobjective, and each character has one. It is the main goal in the character's play life. Everything they do is ultimately so they can fulfill that quest.

Romeo's main objective is to find a new woman and be happy in the relationship. Dorothy from *The Wizard of Oz* wants to find a better place to live.

All characters also have objectives they try to fulfill in each unit of the play (units are discussed later) as they seek to fulfill their main objective.

Romeo must deal with many unit objectives such as: Juliet is a Capulet, Tybolt, banishment, and suicide, before he fulfills his super objective. Dorothy has to deal with getting back to Kansas, finding her way to the Emerald City, getting the witch's broom, and a fake Wizard before she realizes, "there's no place like home."

Because of conflict with others characters, all characters will be forced to abandon their superobjectives at times and struggle to fulfill the unit-by-unit objectives, but they always are working their way back to their superobjectives. Their superobjective is the only reason characters in plays exist.

As they string along the unit-by-unit objectives, they move through the play never forgetting their quest to fulfill their superobjective. Sometimes they fulfill the unit objectives and move on to the next unit, and sometimes they don't fulfill the unit objectives because they are forced by other characters to move on to the next unit. They should never look back to past unit objectives. Always look to fulfill the superobjective, and to get there the character must seek to fulfill the unit objectives.

The film *Little Miss Sunshine* illustrates this very well. Each one of the characters has very strong superobjectives, and as they are all united in the cross-country voyage, they deal with unit objectives, never forgetting to try and fulfill their superobjective.

The characters in Sondheim's *Into the Woods* also illustrate this point very well. Each character has a very strong superobjective, and as they romp through the woods, they have to deal with many unit objectives, but none of them ever forget their superobjective. And in the end, all have successfully fulfilled their super objectives—at least at the end of act one.

Dramatic Action

What is dramatic action? Why is it different from action? Is there a difference? Understanding the dramatic action in a play is a major key to faithfully interpreting the script.

Dramatic action is action with a purpose. It is characters doing things that fulfill purpose/objectives and not just doing actions/things the playwright needs them to do to support the play's themes.

There was a commercial on TV that was selling a fast-food burger. It had two young men in their late teens, early twenties. One guy's objective was to buy a new car; the other's was to get something to eat at the fast-food joint. As the car buyer was looking at vehicles on a used car lot, each time he would say something about a car he was admiring, the other guy would compare it to how great the burger was. So the one guy would say, "I like these leather seats." The other's response was, "Me too, we'd both look great sitting on them eating a warm double cheeseburger with steamy bacon on top." Not once did the commercial have a voice-over saying that the burger place had the best burgers in the business. It was implied through characters fulfilling objections with dramatic action.

A student wrote a play with a plot about rich men purchasing Pilipino mail-order brides for sexual favors and how the men used these women. The student hated these rich men for doing it and had many characters saying what terrible human beings these rich guys were. They were doing actions, but there wasn't any dramatic action showing the audience how terrible these men were. The characters were only spouting what the playwright wanted them to say to illustrate her theme. Their actions didn't have character purpose.

The TV commercial had dramatic action... the Pilipino play didn't.

For other examples of dramatic action, refer to my textbook *Scriptwriting Structure: To the Point Pointers*.

PASTO Is Not a Dish at an Italian Restaurant

PASTO is an anagram for a theory on play structure. If it were served at an Italian restaurant, it would be the number one item on the menu among playwrights and directors. When I was in the MFA playwriting program at UNLV, this theory was the Bible in play structure. It has not only helped me as a playwright but with my directing also.

The letters signify:

P — preparation
A — attack
S — struggle
T — turn
O — outcome

PASTO comes from an out-of-print playwriting book titled *Primer of Playwriting* by Kenneth MacGowan. Over my teaching years, I have connected PASTO to Aristotle's four components of play structure. But I like PASTO better because of the "A"—attack.

Aristotle's four components of play structure are: exposition, conflict, climax, and denouement. Putting PASTO and the four components side by side would look like this:

Exposition	Preparation/Attack
Conflict	Struggle
Climax	Turn
Denoument	Outcome

Let's define/dissect each of the components using *The Wizard of Oz* as the corpse play.

Exposition / Preparation: The who, what, when, where, and why. Dorothy, a twelve-year-old orphan girl, living in rural Kansas with her aunt and uncle, during the Depression, spring, unhappy with her life.

Attack: The attack is when the major dramatic question (MDQ) is asked. It is when the audience finds out what is at stake in the play. It is why the audience is interested in the play. Most people think the MDQ of *The Wizard of Oz* is: Will Dorothy find her way home? But that's not it. That question is asked too late in the script to be the MDQ.

Ready, Set, MDQ

When should the MDQ be asked in a play? The point of attack has changed over the years. In Shakespeare's plays (which are five acts), the MDQ is always asked at the end of the first act.

Let's look at *Romeo and Juliet*. The show opens with a conflict between the Montagues and Capulets. A question is asked: Will they stop feuding? But that is not the MAJOR dramatic question.

The next scene is Benvolio with Romeo's parents. He says, "I'll know his grievance or be much denied." He is going to find out what is wrong with Romeo, but again that is not the MDQ.

The next couple of scenes introduce the Capulets. After a short scene between Lord Capulet and Paris, Juliet, her mom, and the nurse are discovered. The mother asks Juliet:

> "Marry that marry is the very theme
> I come to talk of. Tell me daughter Juliet,
> How stands your dispositions to be married?"

Again another question but not the major one. Back to Romeo and his buddies as they talk about crashing the Capulet party because they all want to meet a girl. Will they meet some women is a question but not the MDQ. Romeo and Juliet meet, fall in love, and at the end of the first act as Romeo is leaving the party, the nurse says to Juliet:

"His name is Romeo, and a Montague;
The only son of your great enemy."

Juliet says:

"My only love sprung from my only hate,
Too early seen unknown, and known too late!
Prodigious birth of love it is to me,
That I must love a loathed enemy."

And with that the MDQ is set as: Will Romeo and Juliet's love survive?

In modern playwriting, the MDQ is not set so late. It should be set within the first few minutes of the play. Or by the 10 percent point in the script.

The MDQ in *The Wizard of Oz* is: Will Dorothy find a better place to live? And it's set in the song, "Somewhere Over the Rainbow."

Pippin (Schwartz and Hirson)

The MDQ in *Pippin* is: Will Pippin find something to satisfy him in his life? And it is set in the song, "Corner of the Sky."

I see a pattern beginning here. In musicals, the MDQ is usually asked in a song.

In television and film scripts, the MDQ is asked at different points in the scripts. In a full-length film script, the MDQ is asked about ten minutes in. The person who taught me this said, "You can set your watch to when the MDQ is asked in films." And since I heard that statement twenty-five years ago, I am amazed at how accurate those words are. The next time you're watching a film, check your watch at the beginning, usually after the credits, and check it again when you know what the MDQ of the film is. I guarantee it'll be right around ten minutes if not right on the dot.

Check the time when Dorothy sings "Somewhere Over the Rainbow" in the film.

In TV, it depends on the length of the show. If it is a half-hour sitcom, the MDQ is usually asked within the first two or three lines—or during the teaser.

My wife loved the TV series *Seinfeld*. One of her favorite episodes was set around the cast losing their car in a parking deck. The MDQ was set right away with: Will they find the car? Many things happened as they searched for the car that made the episode a classic, and it ended when they found the car.

Another Serving of PASTO

Conflict / Struggles: The core of all plays is conflict. It's all the dramatic action the characters take to fulfill their objectives and ultimately answer the MDQ.

In the original PASTO, I was taught the *S* was struggle. But as I shared this theory over the years in my classes, I realized that there was more than one struggle that characters faced to fulfill the MDQ, so I added the "s" and it became struggles.

Everything Dorothy does in *The Wizard of Oz*, from trying to get home before the tornado, to trying to pick the apples from the trees, to crossing the poppy field, to getting the broom from the Wicked Witch, are all struggles.

Climax / Turn: When the MDQ is answered. The climactic scene in *Oz* where the MDQ of "Will she find a better place to live?" is answered when Dorothy is clicking her heels together and saying, "There's no place like home." And when she gets back home, she realizes that there isn't any better place to live than where she is.

Denouement / Outcome: The wrapping up of the loose ends. Dorothy is discovered in bed back home, surrounded by her family and friends, and she says how happy she is to be where she is.

Sometimes plays don't have an outcome. Audiences are left with P. A. S. T. The "O" or what happens next is left up to the audience to decide.

There isn't an *O* in the film *Butch Cassidy and the Sundance Kid*. There is a freeze-frame at the end of the film when the two are shot.

Sometimes plays have an outcome that is too long. I wrote an adaptation of *The Three Little Pigs* that was set on Old MacDonald's farm. Old MacDonald was trying to find new homes for all his animals because he had lost his farm to Reaganomics. He was successful in achieving his objective for all the animals. For the three little pigs, he gave them each a small sum of money, which they used to build their respective straw, stick, and brick houses. Old MacDonald and the mother sow of the three little pigs went on tour winning blue ribbons on the county fair circuit. The plot follows the traditional story as the Big Bad Wolf destroys the straw and stick homes but can't blow the brick house down. The climax takes place as all the farm animals reunite at a county fair and defeat the Big Bad Wolf. This involved a chase through the audience that had the children who attended very excited.

This fever-pitch scene was followed by Old MacDonald telling the audience what each of the animals was doing "now." During the first performance, I didn't think the actor playing Old MacDonald was going to make it through the monologue. The children were not interested in anything he had to say. The play was over; the Big Bad Wolf had been defeated. The audience didn't really care because there was nothing at stake. The MDQ had been answered. They just wanted to leave the theatre and discuss what they had just seen.

I rewrote the ending before the second performance of the day, cutting the monologue down to just a few sentences, and the play worked so much better. The kids all left the theatre excited and talking about the show. The long monologue would have killed that excitement.

This illustrates how denouement/outcome should wrap up the loose ends as quickly as possible.

For examples of scripts with the denouement/outcome too long, see my textbook *Scriptwriting Structure: To-the-Point Pointers*.

Action Divided into Units

Plays are written in acts. They might be a five-act play or a three-act play, a two-act, or even a one-act play. Many times those acts are divided into scenes.

And as a director, it's your job to make sure scenes are broken into even smaller divisions called units to fully understand the action of the play and the spine of each character.

Constantine Stanislavski, a Russian director, working around 1900, was the first to label these smaller divisions units. He went on to say that units could be divided into beats. Beats are the different ways characters try to fulfill unit objectives. Just remember that each unit and each beat has an objective the character is trying to fulfill as they seek to fulfill their super objective.

Let's say that I want to borrow five dollars from you. To illustrate beats within units, let's have you just saying "no" to every beat of the unit.

ME
May I borrow five dollars?

YOU
No.

ME
I really need five dollars.

                    YOU
No.

                    ME
If I don't get the money, I will die.

                    YOU
No.

                    ME
Are you my best friend?

                    YOU
No, you can't have the money.

                    ME
I loaned you five bucks when you needed it.

                    YOU
Sorry, no.

                    ME
If you don't give me the five bucks I'll break your arm.

                    YOU
No.

                    ME
Forget it, I don't need your stinkin' money. I'm going to the baseball game.

I went about trying to get the five bucks (my objective) several different ways. I asked nicely, I begged, I worked on your sympathy, I tried to guilt you into giving it to me, and I threatened you. Each one of those things I did, the beat in the unit changed. When I finally gave up and moved on, the unit changed.

Usually a character is not going to try those different avenues with only one line. They will exhaust each attempt before moving on to the next. Romeo meets Benvolio after the opening conflict between the Montagues and Capulets. After the fight, Benvolio is in a scene with Romeo's parents. They are asking him what is wrong with their son. He's not sure, but when he sees Romeo coming into the scene, he asks the parents to leave and he'll find out what wrong. The unit changes there because his objective changes. Make sure you always illustrate unit changes with a movement.

My book *Scriptwriting Structure: To-the-Point Pointers* has a magical explanation of Stanislavski's teachings on units.

Quilters (Newman and Damashak)

Each unit contains a wealth of information that will help you better understand the structure, meaning, and mood of the play. It is your job as director to interpret each unit and find this critical information. For an in-depth list of all the information you should have for each unit, see the section, "The Bible of Directing."

Visually Show What is Verbally Happening

The theatre is a visual art. I sat next to a guy at the Barbican Theatre in London (The National Theatre of England) at a performance of *Hamlet* in which Daniel Day-Lewis was playing the title role and Dame Judy Dench was playing Gertrude. Both their performances and the show were something that I'll never forget! This guy sitting next to me had an open text of *Hamlet* on his lap, and he was reading the words as the actors delivered them. He didn't see one moment of the brilliant performances of either the Academy Award-winning actors or the rest of the cast.

That's too bad. Not only did they deliver wonderful performances of the entire text, they were also incredible to watch in their actions and performances. The text reader made sure they said the lines faithfully, but he could have listened to an audio recording of the show. He missed that they also told the story visually through their movement and actions (blocking and gestures).

Unfortunately, most plays that I see forget that the theatre is a visual art. Bad theatre is a group of actors standing center stage talking and none of them are moving. As I said in the Introduction, the director's most important job is to interpret the playwright's words. And that is accomplished by visually showing what is verbally happening.

Visual Storytelling: *A Flea in Her Ear* (Feydeau)

I can walk toward my wife as I say, "I love you," or move away from her as I say those same three words. The movement I take tells a lot about my true feelings. Just as my wife knows what I truly mean because of my movement, an audience learns the same thing. The blocking, along with the "subtext," interprets the playwright's words.

Blocking Should Reflect the Subtext

What is subtext?

In my book, *Postcard Pointers to the Performer*, subtext is an entire chapter titled, "Cussing Subtext." In a nutshell, subtext is the unspoken words a character is really saying even though they are saying other words.

The following is an excerpt from my acting book *Postcard Pointers to the Performer* (Dominion Publications):

> *I am walking down the main boulevard of the university campus, and I see a friend. I say, "Hi, how are you?"*
>
> *The friend responds in a sour, negative way. "I'm fine!"*
>
> *If I take my friend at face value of his words, I would respond, "Glad to hear that you are doing fine," and we would continue to walk away from one another.*
>
> *But because I care about my friend and read/hear his subtext, I ask, "What's wrong?"*
>
> *He responds sourly for the second time, "Nothing."*
>
> *Again, if I react to what he just said to me... that "nothing" is wrong, I should continue to walk away, and that would be the end of our conversation.*
>
> *But I don't, and once again I ask, "What's wrong?"*
>
> *Why do I do that? Because I heard my friend's subtext. I knew something was wrong because of the way he said, "I'm fine," and "Nothing." I read his subtext, and I know that something was bothering him.*

Blocking that supports the subtext of the characters is one of the many tools a director employs to support

Blocking supporting subtext: *Company* (Sondheim and Furth)

the playwright's words and character objectives. The movement should reflect the subtext.

I can say, "I love you," and move not only the two ways mentioned above, but there are three different moves I can do as I say it. The movement will illustrate what I truly mean—the subtext. I can say those words and stand still, I can say them and move away, or I can move toward the person as I say them. If I were neutral about my love, I wouldn't move. If I don't meant that I love you, I would walk away. If the character truly loves the person, then he would move toward that character. There are many other variations on how to say I love you, but those three illustrate how the blocking supports the true meaning of the dialogue.

The movement should visually show what is verbally happening. Let's say one character is belittling or controlling another. The dominant character could circle the other character that is cowering, just like an animal circles its prey.

When I directed *The Tiger* by Murray Schisgal, I had the male character (the Tiger) in the script jump from furniture piece to furniture piece throughout the play, just like a cat does around the house.

In a play I critiqued for a former student, a family is split over something one of the siblings did. In the climactic scene of the show, I suggested the two factions stand on opposite sides of the bed in a hospice as they argue literally over the dying body of the brother.

An exercise I use in my directing class to illustrate this important point is this: Stage/block a scene with dialogue, and then run the scene without the dialogue, and see if the scene tells the same story through the blocking, visually without the dialogue.

You have to visually tell the story or visually say what is verbally happening. Remember, the theatre is a visual art. If you're not telling the story visually and the actors are just standing around talking… you might as well be doing radio.

The designers have given their input, and it's your job to tell the story from the things they have given you. What things am I taking about? The most important thing from the set designer is the ground plan.

Ground Plans and Obstacle Courses are Kissing Cousins

If I am going to Disney World, I get a map of the park. It has the layout of the park, and from it I can get where I want to go. If there are certain rides I want to experience or other things I want to do, I look at the map of the park, plot my route to the rides, and then I work my way through the park as I fulfill my objective.

After reading the script that you are directing, a Disney World that reflects the dramatic action of the play must be created. The ground plan is that world where the characters of the play live. Just as it's not easy to get to the various rides at Disney World because of other people in the park, the paths you must follow, and distractions along the route, your script's ground plan should reflect those obstacles.

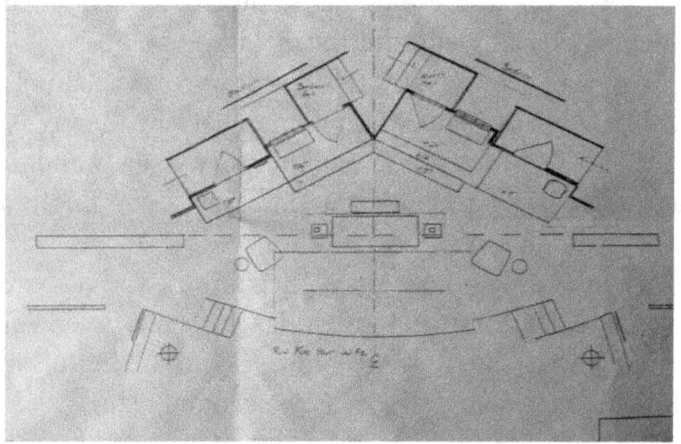

Floor Plan: *Run for Your Wife* (Cooney)

Drama is conflict. To avoid climactic situations too soon, you need an obstacle course that the characters in the play can interact in. If I can get to you and strangle you, the play is over. But if there are obstacles that characters can hide behind, climb on, throw, push, or use as a barrier, climax can be avoided.

Those obstacles can be chairs, sofas, tables, tree stumps, anything that would fit into the environment of the world of the play.

A good ground plan is the foundation to successful blocking, and it will help you with the other tools of directing.

Focus: Who Has the Ball

To put focus on the show, you (the director) must stage/block the show. Don't leave it up to the actors to come up with their own blocking/movement. It's the director's job to put focus on the show.

In a tennis game, the spectators follow the ball. Watch how the heads of the entire audience move together as the game plays out. It's the same with blocking. The movement is telling the story, and you are creating that same kind of focus on the play as it unfolds. The audience must follow who has the ball/focus. Don't drop it.

Movement is the strongest way to put the focus where you want the audience to look, but it always doesn't have to be the actors walking from place to place or sitting or standing.

I once had actors throw a pillow to each other to show the focus, just like a tennis ball. At the end of each line, the speaking actor threw the pillow to the next actor that spoke, and then when that actor's line was finished, they threw the pillow to the next person that spoke.

Movement is also the best way to illustrate unit changes. Sitting is like putting a period at the end of a unit, or standing could show the attack of a new unit.

There are other things you can do to put focus where you want it. If all the characters on stage are looking at one character, that act puts the focus on the character all the others are looking at. It is called eye focus.

If one or more characters point to another character, that will throw the focus to the character being pointed at. That is called line focus. Combining eye and line focus along with levels will only strengthen the focus.

Eye Focus: *Beanie and the Bamboozling Book Machine* (May, Booth, Tibbetts)

Line Focus: *Joseph and the Amazing Technicolor Dreamcoat* (Lloyd-Webber, Rice)

Eye and Line Focus: *Jack and Bella: From Beanstalk to Broadway* (May, Bradford, Owings)

The Triangle Theory

Triangle: *The Fantasticks* (Jones and Schmidt)

Straight lines are a director's worst enemy. They are flat and visually boring. As characters move, they are constantly creating new compositions, and each composition or picture should be some variation of a triangle. The triangles don't have to be just with actors, they can include furniture and other stage pieces in those pictures/triangles.

Remember what I said in the Introduction: On any stage, but especially a proscenium stage, a director paints a picture just as a painter does on a canvas or a photographer does with film. Triangles give stage pictures depth. Straight lines flatten stage pictures. That is true on any type of stage, not just proscenium stages.

Triangle: *Elson: The First Christmas Elf* (May)

Give Me Levels and Lots of Them

Remember, visually show what is verbally happening. Levels can help the blocking tell the story. And not just levels created by the set. The actor can stand, sit, kneel, or lay down to show many levels.

One actor can cower as another stands over the cowering figure. It's obvious who has the focus in a situation like that. But a good set design/ground plan should always include many levels to help visually tell the story too.

Levels: *Working* (Schwartz)

In the Arthur Miller show *The Creation of the World and Other Business*, there is a confrontation between God and Lucifer that is the climax of the play.

To visually show this battle, the set designer had given me lots of levels to work with. Upstage center there was an eight-foot platform that we called heaven. To the stage left side of this platform there was a staircase leading up to heaven. At downright, there was a platform about four feet off the ground. At stage left, there was another platform around two feet off the ground. So, not only did I have the eight-foot, four-foot, and two-foot platforms, but all the variables in between with steps and other heights leading to the three high points.

Set design for first production of *The Creation of the World and Other Business* (Miller)

I directed the show a second time with a similar concept. This show had more color in it.

Set design for second production of *The Creation of the World and Other Business* (Miller)

As the confrontation between God and Lucifer unfolded, I illustrated which character was winning the battle by using the various levels on set. Beat by beat, the winner was always on the higher platform throughout the set. And in the end, God wins. God is on the highest level, Lucifer the next, and Adam, Eve, and Cain are on the stage level.

The ending battle in the first production of *The Creation of the World and Other Business* (Miller)

An actor's movements are only part of the big picture in visually telling the story.

The ending battle in the second production of *The Creation of the World and Other Business* (Miller)

Stage pictures and composition are the end results of blocking. Think of stage pictures and composition as an exclamation point at the end of a sentence. Your movement patterns should result in unit-ending pictures that tell the story. The phrase "A picture is worth a million words" is so true in the theatre.

Composition and Picturization are Kin

Yes, a picture is worth a thousand words. Need I say any more? I refer back to the section, "Visually Show What is Verbally Happening." The composition you create on stage can relate multitudes of messages to the audience. As simple as one actor towering over another on stage, this can tell the audience that the towering figure is winning the battle.

Composition / Picturization: *The Lion in Winter* (Goldman)

Picturization: *Pippin* (Schwartz and Hirson)

As actors move, they are in between compositions. So a show is a constant series of stage picture, blocking, stage picture.

Using techniques like stage areas, levels, body positions, and focus makes composition. Picturization is the final result of making a composition. It tells a story.

Who's Winning the Battle

In the past two sections, I have referred to "who is winning the battle."

Don't forget that the core of all drama is conflict, so what I mean by saying "who is winning the battle" is, after breaking the script into units and beats, you should be able to graph out who is winning the confrontations (the battles) between characters throughout each unit as they are in conflict trying to fulfill their respective objectives.

Winning the battle: *Beanie and the Bamboozling Book Machine* (May, Tibbetts, Booth)

In other words, each beat in every unit has a character that is winning the battle/conflict between the characters in the unit. One character doesn't win all the battles—the play would be boring if that happened. Units will change when one character takes control of the unit or is winning the battle. Movement will help illustrate that. Composition tells the bigger picture.

The character winning the battle will be advancing on the character that is losing. The losing character will be retreating, putting as many obstacles (set pieces) between him/her and the character advancing.

Stage Areas

A proscenium stage can be divided into six areas, three across the back/upstage part of the stage, three across the middle, and three across the downstage part of the stage.

The reason the back part of the stage is called upstage is because stages used to be raked. The back part of the stage was higher than the front, and an actor had to literally walk upstage to get back there. The rake was so the audience who was sitting or standing on a flat area could see actors in the back. In modern theatres, the stage has been flattened and the audience is now raked.

The six stage areas are shown in the diagram below.

UR	UC	UL
R	C	L
DR	DC	DL

Stage areas on a proscenium stage

Right and left is determined by the actor's right and left as they face the audience. The strongest of these areas is down center and the second strongest area would be down right because people read from left to right. The third strongest area is down left. The center three sections are the next strongest and the back three after that. Keeping that in mind, the strongest entrance a character can make is from down right.

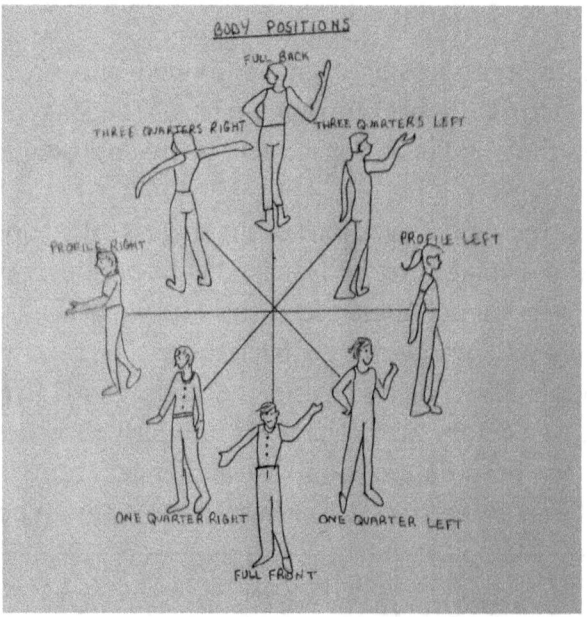

Body positions on a proscenium stage

Going along with stage areas, I should mention actor's body positions. How an actor stands on a proscenium stage can say a lot about who is winning the battle, putting focus where you want it, and supporting the playwright's words. There are nine body positions.

They are full front, one-quarter right or left, profile right or left, three-quarter right or left, and full back.

Full front is the strongest of the positions, one-quarter is next, and as the list goes so goes the strength.

The diagram above illustrates these positions.

Preblock

Always preblock the show before you begin rehearsal. Don't waste the actor's time by blocking on the fly at rehearsal. It's your job to put focus, tell story, make compositions, paint pictures, and keep the tempo moving. If you go into each blocking rehearsal knowing where you want the actors to move and be, it saves so much time.

Blocking: *West Side Story* (Laurents, Bernstein, Sondheim)

I've worked with directors who let the actors do their own movement. Some actors are experienced enough to do that, but it's very rare that you have a cast full of actors with that quality.

If you dictate all the moves, then they are consistent. Your moves should be telling story, and that will help actors develop their characters and strengthen your concept.

Don't make up the blocking at rehearsal. That just wastes everyone's time. Know where you want your actors to be moving, and don't forget to create stage pictures that tell a story.

Don't use the movement that is in many of the acting edition scripts you get from publishers. More than likely, your set design and floor plan are not the same as the set used in the Broadway production, and those moves were taken from the blocking used in the Broadway premiere production of the script.

The Bible of Directing

As I have stressed in previous sections, do your homework, analyze the script, and preblock. And the best place to keep all this information is in the bible of directing, the gospel according to you (the director)— the prompt book.

For my prompt books, if a script is on 8 ½ x 11 paper I reduce the size of the script to 70 percent on a photocopier. That makes it about the same size as any standard acting addition script. I like to put the script in a 9 x 7 x 1-inch plastic, three-ring binder. That size fits nicely into a typical bookshelf. If the text of the script is only on one side the page, the back of each page will serve as the space to write blocking; the blocking will be on the left side of the prompt book, and the text will be on the right.

If you are using a script from any of the play publishers, the first thing you will have to do is disassemble the script and separate it so each page is one sheet. Then insert a blank page in between each page of the script for blocking notes. Let's say that the first page of a script is page two and the back is page three. The blocking notes will be to the left of page two and to the right for page three. When you turn the page of the blocking notes for page three, the backside of that page (now on the left) becomes the page for blocking notes for page four on the right.

Number each move in the script exactly where you want it to happen. Then on the blocking page, write the number and the movement or action you want to happen. With each page, start with the number one. The numbers are not continuous from page to page. I circle all my numbers.

Write all blocking notes in pencil. That way if a move changes, you can erase it and insert the new move, keeping the prompt book up to date. I find it easier to use symbols when I write my blocking out. It saves time.

50 • THE PROCESS OF PLAY DIRECTING

Some that I use are:

X	cross	@	transition
2	"to" as in move to	⊕	sit
↑	stand	//	pause
↺	turn	U	upstage

So if I write ↑ X 2 DR ⊕, that means stand, cross to down right and sit. Use these symbols or make up your own. The following is from a prompt book that I used for a play I directed:

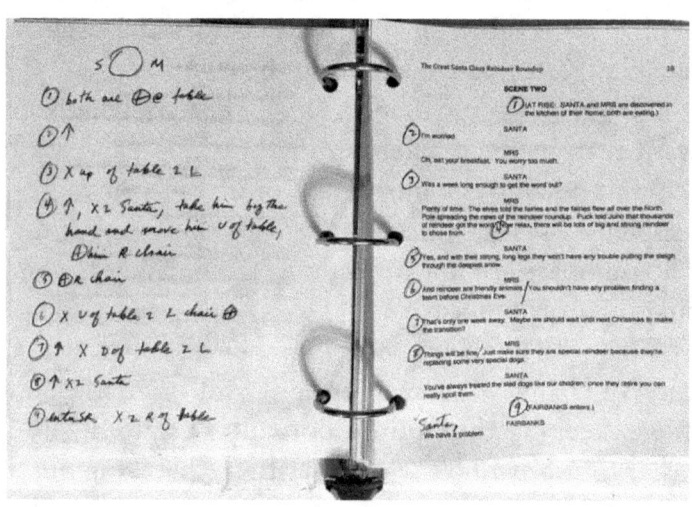

Blocking from the prompt book for *The Great Santa Claus Reindeer Roundup* (May)

Mark all unit and beat changes in the script. They will dictate blocking, tempo, and mood changes.

As mentioned earlier, each unit contains a wealth of information to help interpret the script.

Here is a list of things to jot down in your prompt book for each unit.
- Name each unit. What is its purpose for being in the play? Is it an introductive unit (for the locale, for a character), does it set mood, give background information, etc.
- What is the objective for each character in the unit? Remember unit objectives from the earlier unit objective section.

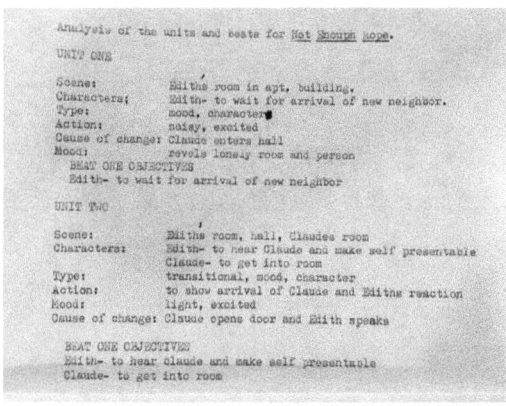

Unit information from the prompt book for *Not Enough Rope* (May)

- What is the tempo for each unit? Make a side-by-side graph of each illustrating what the tempo looks like. Use lines that resemble those on a lie detector or a heart monitor. It is amazing how much this will tell you about the feel of the show.
- What is the mood for each unit? Use an adjective or an image.
- What caused the unit to change?

The beginning of each unit is marked in the script along with the beats. This is illustrated in the next figure. Units are marked in black ink and beats in blue. The red letters mark where light and sound cues are located. The black-circled numbers indicate where blocking movement happens.

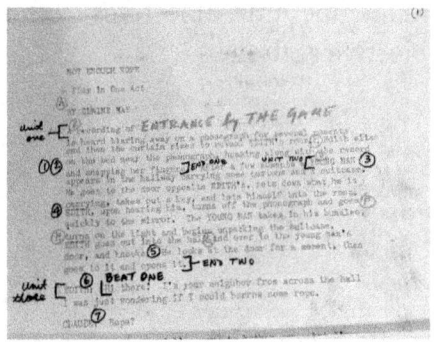

Units, beats, lights, sound, and blocking markings for
Not Enough Rope (May)

When answering the preparation part of PASTO (who, what, when, where, and why) mentioned in the "PASTO is Not a Dish at an Italian Restaurant" section, it is important to note these answers in the prompt script. Here is a list of questions that you should have answers for about each script you are directing.

What happened previous to the beginning of the script?

What is the geographical location? Characters in the south act differently than someone in New York City. The characters in *The Dining Room* act like people from

New England. Could that play take place in any other part of the country? Maybe in the south.

What year does the action take place? The way of the world was different in 1950 compared to 2015. The season (fall, winter, spring, summer) plays an important part in people's lives too. Is it day or night?

How rich or poor are the characters? What is their social environment?

Are they political? Religious? Which religion?

How does the title of the play tie into its meaning? Is it a literal title or metaphorical one? *Cat on a Hot Tin Roof* is a metaphorical title.

Put all costume, set, prop, and sound notes in this book too. Have a copy of the rehearsal schedule and a contact list in the book.

I always include a character entrance/exit graph for all shows I direct, especially for musicals or shows with large casts. It helps to illustrate what characters are in which scene.

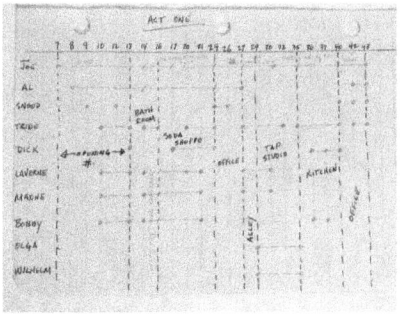

Entrance/Exit graph for *Trixie True Teen Detective* (Hamilton)

List each character's name to the left on a sheet of paper. The page numbers are listed across the top of the graph. A dotted black line runs up and down at the page numbers where each scene begins and ends. I use red dots to indicate on which page each character enters and exits. Then I use red lines connecting the dots to show how long the character is on stage.

By looking in between the black dotted lines, you can see who is in each scene. I have also named each scene by locale. This is a helpful tool when making a rehearsal schedule.

As you can see from this section, the prompt book is more than just a record of the blocking. It is a place where everything is in the same place, and whenever there is a question the answer can be found in the bible of directing—the prompt book.

CHAPTER 3

Rehearsal

I usually don't like to rehearse a full-length show for more than four, maybe five weeks. I am referring to community or educational theatre rehearsal periods of three hours a night, Monday through Friday.

I have a theory that if you have four weeks to rehearse, the actors won't really get serious and get down to work until three weeks in. Three weeks—two weeks in. Two weeks—one week in. A week—four days in. What I'm saying is, don't over rehearse the show. The actors will only get bored with it.

Rehearsing a show for eight weeks takes the life out of it. The actors get bored, and by the time opening night comes around, they have passed their peak.

Start all rehearsals on time. If the rehearsal is supposed to start at seven o'clock, then make sure you are working at seven o'clock so that any actors who walk in after that see that you are working.

I worked at one university theatre where rehearsal was supposed to begin at seven, but it never began until 7:20 or later. Eventually the actors figured out that nothing was going to happen until 7:20, so they began to show up even later than that.

The first show I directed at this university was a disaster getting the actors there on time because they were so used to things starting late. By the second week, the actors had it figured out and all began to show up ten minutes before the scheduled start time, so we could begin on time.

For the first three weeks, take the weekends off, add Saturday in the fourth week, and then don't take any days off for continuity's sake as you roll toward opening night during the final week and a half.

Make sure that you take breaks through the evening, at least one for ten to fifteen minutes at the halfway point in the night. A sample rehearsal schedule is located toward the end of this section.

Rehearsal: *The Fantasticks* (Jones and Schmidt)

Find a Good Stage Manager

A good stage manager makes your directing life much easier. A stage manager worries about things that you shouldn't have to like actors getting to rehearsal on time, having the stage or rehearsal room swept and set for the scenes being rehearsed, and eventually making sure the show runs the way you've conceived it.

I've only touched on the role of the stage manager. There are entire books written about that role. Find a good one and read it. A good stage manager is like a caddy to a golfer. Find a good one and use him or her.

The First Rehearsal / Read-Through

One of the first things you want to do at the first rehearsal is get a contact list started. Most of the information on the contact list can be pulled from audition forms; i.e. address, phone number, and e-mail. But now is the time to get any additional contact information, a second phone number or e-mail address.

At the first rehearsal, take the time to share your concept with the cast, introduce the design staff, and let the designers illustrate how they are going to support the concept. The scenic designer should have a model or renderings of the set. The costume designer should show costumes renderings for each character in the show. The lightning designer should share his/her vision of how he/she will pull all the designs together.

The first read-through is not a polished performance. Don't expect the actors to have their characters developed. That's what rehearsal is for. Don't even correct an actor if they say a word or name of a character incorrectly.

The first read-through is all about letting the actors hear the script read by the actors they will be working with. It's about getting to know one another.

Table Work

I have mixed feeling about table work. I think many directors talk a show to its doom. Don't get me wrong, I always have the first read-through sitting around a table or in a circle of chairs and talk characterization with each actor, but a lot of that can be done when the actor is up and moving during beginning blocking rehearsals.

Keep in mind the movement supports the subtext, and the actor will understand what you think of a character because of the movement and business you give to the character.

Warm-ups

I always figured if rehearsal was not until seven p.m. that people were warmed up both physically and vocally, after all they have been moving and talking all day long. And thus there was no need to do any warm-up exercises. However, I have found that doing some group games before rehearsal helps get everyone energized, sharpened, and focused for rehearsal.

One of my favorites is Big Booty. The cast stands in a circle. One person is Big Booty and the others count off counting from one counterclockwise until each person has a number. The person who is Big Booty begins to chant the words "big booty" four times, establishing the tempo of the game. Start off slow and pick the tempo up as the cast understands how to play the game. So they say:

Big Booty, Big Booty
Big Booty, number two

Big Booty can pick any number he/she wants to pick. Then the person who is number two has to say:

Number two, number five.

The person who is number two can also pick any number he/she wants. In this case, the person who is number five then says:

Number five – and he/she picks another number.

The key is it all has to be said in the tempo that was set by Big Booty. A person can say "Big Booty" instead of a number, and then the Big Booty person has to say, "Big Booty" and another number.

If someone doesn't come in on their number, or if they don't keep the rhythm, they drop out of the circle and each person's number shifts one less if they are to the right of the person who dropped out.

The person who is Big Booty begins a new game and keeps the game moving, while everyone else has to rethink his or her number as the game is being played. The game continues until there are only two people left in the circle and they are the winners.

There are many theatre games. Find the one that works for you. I had to be really selective about which games I used when and on whom in various rehearsals. Some actors resisted them so much that it just wasn't worth my time trying to bully them into opening themselves up. And other exercises changed the timbre of the rehearsal. It was important for me to remember that each exercise is a tool, and you have to be careful about which tool you use. You wouldn't use a saw when you need a hammer, for instance.

Get it Blocked

I really think it's important to get the entire show blocked as quickly as possible. Take the time to stage the entire show before you even start working any part of it. Actors can relate to their character and understand their lines much better when they have the movement supporting the lines. And I can't say it enough, good blocking visually shows what is verbally happening. The blocking will help the actors understand their subtext too. Having movement to associate with what they are saying will also help them memorize their lines. It gives them something to identify with the words and lines.

Divide the script into manageable sections as you begin to block. In a standard acting edition script, ten to fifteen pages is a realistic amount to block each night.

Always run through what has been staged at least once without stopping before you leave for the night. And then run that section again at the beginning of the next night's blocking rehearsal before moving on to any new blocking. Take time to run entire scenes and acts as you crescendo through the blocking rehearsals before moving on to new scenes or acts. That will keep blocked sections of the script fresh in the actors' minds.

Work It

Once the show is completely blocked, it is time to work it. That doesn't mean you haven't made any suggestions during table work or blocking rehearsals, but now is the time to talk through any problems you see as you guide the actors into the performances that support the playwright's words and your concept.

Don't forget to say what's working well too. Critiquing doesn't just mean to correct what isn't working. Pointing out what is working will give actors the confidence they need to create, and they won't just see your directing suggestions as all negative.

Positive and negative coaching is not the task it sounds like. The actors should already be on the same page with you because you've shared your concept, characterizations, and blocking with them previous to these working rehearsals.

A working rehearsal: *The Fantasticks* (Jones and Schmidt)

Again, divide the script into manageable sections to work on. You can get through a lot more of the script than the sections you broke the script into when blocking. Breaking each act in half will be a manageable amount.

Yes, you are looking at character development, unit battles, and objectives. But don't forget tempo. All units should not be played at the same tempo. A good rule of thumb, though, is keep things moving.

A note about giving line readings to actors: I have explained subtext. When an actor is not saying the subtext the way it should be said, it's very easy to give a line reading to them when you talk about the subtext. Be careful. I have found that giving line readings shuts down the creative process. Talk about what produces the response on a problem line. Understanding the given circumstances and the previous line's subtext will help the actor grasp the subtext. Remember to trust your actors.

I only give a line reading as a last resort.

Talk through any and all problems, run the problem section, and move on. And then always end the rehearsal with a run thru of what you have just worked. Don't stop the run for any reason. Let the actors get through it. You can always take notes and talk to the actors after the run.

And then always start the next day's rehearsal with a continuous run of the pages you worked on at the previous day's rehearsal. It keeps things fresh as you crescendo to getting the entire script worked.

Run It

When you get to climatic moments like the end of scenes or act endings, make sure that you run them periodically throughout the "work it" portion of the rehearsal to keep everything fresh.

When you get to the "run it" part of the rehearsal period, let it be that: a run thru. Don't stop things. No matter how bad it looks. Let the actors get a feel for running the section, the act, or the entire show.

You should start taking notes when you get to the run it part of rehearsal. Sit the entire cast down in the audience while you stand in front of them to deliver the notes. Having the entire cast at this process brings them together, and they all can understand what it is you want from others. Yes, you are giving individual acting notes, and that should help everyone when they can hear what you expect form individual actors. You should also be talking about mood, tempo, and interpretation, which affect the entire cast. If a scene or section needs to be run or worked, this is the time to do it. A note session is not only about the things that are not working. By pointing out the things that are working, you will help actors with similar things that are not working.

ACTORS ACTING LIKE DIRECTORS

Remember the feather theory? Actors only have one feather, and they all have the same size feather. They were hired as actors, not directors. It's not good for cast camaraderie if one actor tells another how to act. The message that practice relates to the actor being told what to do is: the one talking is better than they are.

I always begin the rehearsal process by talking about this. I ask the actors not to do it even if one actor asks the advice of another. Everything should be through the eyes of only one director.

It is just not a good idea for actors to direct other actors.

PAPER TECH

Don't be surprised with what your designers are going to do at the first tech. Because of weekly production meetings, the communication channels have always been open, so I don't mean surprised with what they are going to do, but surprised with cue placement. A paper tech is a good way to learn where cues will happen in the script, and it will let the stage manager know where each tech moment throughout the show is going to happen.

This can happen sitting around a table. The designers, the stage manager, and the director are the only ones who need to be in attendance.

TECH WITHOUT ACTORS

You don't need actors hanging around to do a first tech rehearsal with the light, sound, and scene-shift cues. This rehearsal is really to show all the tech staff when, what, and how they are to do all cues. And it also gives the stage manager an opportunity to learn how to call all the cues.

And most importantly, it's a time for you to see what things are going to look like too.

The first tech is usually done as a cue-to-cue. The entire show is not run. Each cue is worked through with all involved, and then the stage manager will move to the next cue. Make sure that you take the time to spike all scenery pieces exactly where you want them to be. Use glow tape on all steps, platforms, and the edge/lip of the stage.

During the curtain call for a show I directed, an actor walked out in the dark on a stage that didn't have glow tape, and he walked off the edge of the stage and broke his ankle.

There are shows where I've used the actors to move the scenery. A tech without actors then means that the actors are there as technicians and not there as actors.

Don't do scene changes in total black. There will always be light coming from somewhere in a theatre (exit signs), and the audience will be able to see the outlines of the people moving the scenery. Use a low intensity blue wash for all scene changes and choreograph them. The audience will see them and they become part of the show (the magic of the theatre).

FIRST TECH WITH ACTORS

Remind the actors that the first tech with them present is for the technicians, just like the first rehearsal was for the actors. The technicians have not been rehearsing for a month. Yes, they've had paper techs, techs without actors, but this is the first time they've put it together with the actors.

Carolyn Strauss as Luisa at tech rehearsal for *The Fantasticks* (Jones and Schmidt)

This tech rehearsal is done as a run thru with all the actors running through the script with the addition of all the cues. There are often many stops as cues are perfected with actors present. This is the rehearsal to take the time and work through any tech problems. Costumes are not worn at this rehearsal. Actors could be sitting and standing around a lot.

Actors frustrated with techies not doing their jobs error-free can create problems only intended for guests on the *Jerry Springer Show*.

I usually have a second tech rehearsal with actors, again not wearing costumes, where I try to get through the show without stopping it for any reason. If there is a major technical problem, I will stop, but I try to let it run.

It is time now to stage the curtain call. And I mean just that—stage it. The curtain call is just as important as the rest of the show. Early in my directing career, I used to end the show with a blackout, keep the lights down until the stage was clear, and then bump the lights back up and begin the curtain call. But a problem with that is, sometimes the lights were down so long that the applause had stopped before the curtain call began. And having the applause stop before the curtain call begins is death to a curtain call.

Curtain call for *Hocus Pocus Horticulture* (May)

I learned a great trick when I saw *Les Miserables* in London in 1986. After the lights faded to black at the end of the show, they were black for only a beat before they were bumped right back up. The actors that were on stage bowed from the place they were sanding when the lights faded. And then with the lights up full, all the members on stage moved to where they would be making their entrance for the curtain call. Meanwhile, the first actors to be bowing were already down center making their bow.

Everything was choreographed and executed right in front of the audience, and it became part of the show. This technique kept the show moving right into the curtain call.

Start your curtain call with the lesser roles and then work your way up to the leads as the last to bow. When bowing, be you, don't bow as the character.

I don't like it when cast members applaud for each other as they are taking a bow. The curtain call is the time for the audience to say thank you to the actors. There is plenty of opportunity for actors to pat themselves on the back in the dressing room after the show. So I make it a rule to not let the actors applaud for other cast members in the show during the curtain call.

As a director, I don't want to be brought on stage during a curtain call and be given anything by the cast either. The audience is not there to see that sort of congratulatory event. That can all take place backstage among cast and crewmembers.

FIRST DRESS REHEARSAL

Or, when actors put on a costume for the first time, they leave their minds in the dressing room. The show is going great. Rehearsals are running smoothly. Everyone has been showing up on time, and rehearsal ends each night on a positive note. Even the tech rehearsals were a breeze.

And then comes the first dress! It is a disaster. Don't worry about it! It seems like it always happens. There is something about actors putting on a costume for the first time that spells disaster. It doesn't matter how long you have rehearsed, this phenomenon is as regular as Santa at Christmas. When actors put on a costume for the first time, they seem to forget most everything that has been rehearsed for the past month.

I have often canceled notes after the dress rehearsal and treated the company to pitchers of beer at a local pub or pizza at the theatre.

I also treat the first dress as a third tech rehearsal. I do not stop for any tech problems, but I will stop if a costume is giving an actor any problems, like the way it fits or if an actor doesn't have time to make a costume change. If there are quick costume changes, the time is taken to choreograph these changes. Make sure you have dressers and the same dresser always does the same actor's changes.

I always try to have at least two dress rehearsals before any preview performances or opening night. If an actor has an unusual costume, like a hoop skirt or if they have to wear boots or high heels, I ask for those costume pieces very early in the rehearsal process when we start running scenes and acts. If a female character has to wear a dress or a skirt in the show, I ask the actor to begin wearing that early in rehearsal too.

Women sit and walk differently in a dress or skirt than they do in jeans. I also don't let actors wear sandals or tennis shoes to rehearsal because people walk differently in sandals and tennis shoes than they do in hard-sole shoes.

Bob May as Byke in *Under the Gaslight* (Jensen)

I once played a villain in an old-fashioned melodrama *Under the Gaslight* where, just two days before the show opened, I was given a cape and some big boots that the character wore. I had been rehearsing in tennis shoes and didn't have a rehearsal cape. I had to totally rethink how the character walked once I put the boots on, and the cape got in my way more than I used it for the first week of performances.

Some directors like to have a costume parade before the first dress rehearsal so they can view the costume with the actor wearing it under the lights that will be used in the scene the costume is worn in. I find that I don't need a parade. I can view the costumes as the first dress is unfolding—no pun intended. I take extensive notes on the costumes. There are usually not many surprises because the costume designer and I have been communicating regularly at the weekly production meetings.

Don't worry. Once the costume gets used to the actor, things will fall into place, and everything will go back to what was happening in rehearsal.

PREVIEWS

Giving an actor a free chance to see how an audience is going to react to what they are doing is like winning the lottery without buying a ticket.

Having a preview with family and friends is not beneficial most of the time. By all means invite them, but also invite people from a homeless shelter, a senior citizen home, or a hospital ward. Yes, an invited audience is probably going to be nice because they are getting to see the show for free, but they will react in ways that will prepare your cast for what a paying audience will do. They will let the cast and crew know when to expect laughs, applause, or when an audience is bored, or when to expect them to throw tomatoes.

SAMPLE REHEARSAL SCHEDULE

To illustrate the rehearsal process, I have included my rehearsal schedule for Neil Simon's *Barefoot in the Park*. We rehearsed the show from June 4 through the opening on July 12 (five and a half weeks). We didn't rehearse on Wednesday nights because of church, but toward the end of the rehearsal period, Wednesday nights were included.

WEEK ONE

Monday, June 4	7pm Read-thru table work
Tuesday, June 5	7pm Block pg 1-13 to Mother's entrance
Wednesday, June 6	OFF
Thursday, June 7	7pm Run pg 1-13
	8pm Block pg 13-25
Friday, June 8	7pm Run pg 13-25
	8pm Block pg 26-39 Act II Scene I
Saturday, June 9	OFF
Sunday, June 10	7pm Run Act I

WEEK TWO

Monday, June 11	7pm Run pg 26-39
	8pm Block pg 39-52 Act II Scene 2
Tuesday, June 12	7pm Run Act II
	8:30pm Block pg 53-70 Act III
Wednesday, June 13	OFF
Thursday, June 14	7pm Run pg 53-70
	8pm Work pg 1-13
Friday, June 15	7pm Run pg 1-13
	8pm Work pg 13-25
Saturday, June 16	OFF
Sunday, June 17	7pm Run Act I

WEEK THREE

Monday, June 18	7pm Work pg 26-39
	9pm Run pg 26-39
Tuesday, June 19	7pm Work pg 39-52
	9pm Run pg 39-52
Wednesday, June 20	OFF
Thursday, June 21	7pm Run Act II
	9pm Work pg 53-70
Friday, June 22	7pm Run pg 53-70
Saturday, June 23	OFF
Sunday, June 24	7pm Run-through

WEEK FOUR

Monday, June 25	7pm Run/Work Act I
Tuesday, June 26	7pm Run/Work Act II
Wednesday, June 27	7pm Run/Work Act III
Thursday, June 28	7pm Run-through
Friday, June 29	7pm Run-through
Saturday, June 30	OFF
Sunday, July 1	OFF

WEEK FIVE

Monday, July 2	7pm Run Act I
Tuesday, July 3	7pm Run Act II
Wednesday, July 4	7pm TBA
Thursday, July 5	7pm Run Act III
Friday, July 6	7pm Run-through
Saturday, July 7	7pm Run-through
Sunday, July 8	4pm Tech

WEEK SIX

Monday, July 9	6pm Tech/Dress
Tuesday, July 10	6pm Call
	7pm Dress
Wednesday, July 11	6pm Call
	7pm Preview Run
Thursday, July 12	6pm Call
	7pm Opening Night

I handed this rehearsal schedule out at the first rehearsal and stuck with it through the entire rehearsal period without any changes.

PERFORMANCES

Performance is what it's all about. You've been working for this moment throughout rehearsal. The time has finally come. The last element will be added;

76 • THE PROCESS OF PLAY DIRECTING

you're ready to let your baby be seen by a paying audience. Theatre doesn't exist without an audience.

For me, the first performance is always the best performance because of the excitement of opening night. I realize it's not the best. There are better performances in the run because actors learn so much from playing in front of an audience night after night. But for me, nothing ever equals that opening night feeling and rush.

And then be prepared for the opening night letdown.

Performance: *The Fantasticks* (Jones and Schmidt)

THE OPENING NIGHT LETDOWN

As collaborative artists, we have all worked together for a successful opening night. We have all spent a lot of time together creating a work of art. As a director, you have put in more time than anyone else. Long before you talked to designers or had auditions, you were analyzing the script.

Opening night should be a triumphant, happy time. And it usually is, especially if the show is a hit. But don't be suicidal when you experience a letdown, this feeling of abandonment. It happens after opening night when you realize your job is over.

Yes, you can always continue to attend performances and give notes to the actors, but your baby has been born and you realize it can live without you, and the surrogate mother, the stage manger, is keeping your baby alive now. Once the show opens, your baby no longer needs you. The actors are hang gliding into wonderful new flights of discovery with audience reactions.

The actors will experience this letdown when the show is over.

BRUSH-UP REHEARSALS

Many theatres run shows for multiple weekends, and if there are only performances on Friday, Saturday, and Sunday, that means the cast is off more days than they perform.

The question is, should there be a brush-up rehearsal on the Thursday night before performances begin again for the next week? I have mixed feelings about one. I think it can be helpful if they are treated seriously. Too many times I have had them where it was a waste of time, even when I was there and had my serious face on.

I have found several other things that work just as well as a full-blown brush-up rehearsal. One, have the cast do a speed run through of the lines, without any acting or feeling. Two, come in a half hour earlier than the call time on Friday night and run various scenes on stage before the house opens.

If doing a musical, run some of the musical numbers, especially the ones with big dance numbers. That gets the juices flowing once again.

The brush-up is also a very good time to take archive photos of the production. Make a list so you don't waste anyone's time. Shoot in the order from beginning to end. I always like the photos to be shot with the lighting used in the show, and by shooting in order, the light board operator just moves forward through the cues.

CHAPTER 4

Tips

These tips don't fall under the first three chapters, but they are just as important. They're not in any specific order.

Read the book *Backwards and Forwards*

It's a small book with a big message. It's written by David Ball and published by Southern Illinois University Press. I hope to achieve with this directing book what Mr. Ball did with his book for script analysis. He was brief and to the point.

I'm just a director, not a god

This topic was briefly touched on in Chapter One. As an opening night gift, I was given a T-shirt that read, "I'm Just a Director, Not a God... but I completely understand how you could be confused." Unfortunately, some directors believe this statement.

Just because you are the director, that doesn't mean you are God. It doesn't say anywhere in the Bible that God created directors as supreme beings!

Yes, as a director you are in control, but remember that you are only as good as the collaboration you have with the actors and designers you are working with. Don't ever forget that the theatre is a collaborative art.

Success is very regional, and you'll find that you are always "the best director" with the actors you are currently working with.

What I'm saying is, just because you are directing, don't get a big head. Without talented designers, actors, and technicians to fulfill your vision, you are just a director who dreams of a perfect production.

A good script and talented actors are 99 percent of directing

I don't have any actual facts backing up the percentage I am using to title this tip, but I'd bet big money in Vegas that if I am directing a show that has a good script, and I have talented actors supporting me… the show will be successful.

It doesn't matter how talented you think you are or that you may be the next Harold Prince. Without a good script and talented actors, you are only a director with a lot of concepts that your collaborators can't comprehend.

Directing is so much easier when you are working with talented designers and intelligent, thinking actors who understand your concept and work just as hard as you do to fulfill your directorial image.

Form Bonds

When you find a talent... don't lose it.

The percentage of talented working professionals in this business is lower than the old maids found in a bag of cooked Orville Redenbacher popcorn. Form a bond when you find talent.

I must also say in the same breath—never close yourself off to new talent. At an audition, I can tell within the first few seconds if a person has any talent. Talented actors seem to stand out like reflective road signs at night when a bright light encounters them.

You'll know talent when it shines on you.

Don't waste an actor's time

As an actor, I always resented when I had to go to rehearsal and I was not used. I swore when I directed I would never waste any actor's time. Make a schedule for the entire rehearsal period, give it to the cast and crew at the first rehearsal, and stick to it. If you find that you have fallen behind or gotten ahead, revise the schedule.

Happy actors tend to be more productive at rehearsal.

Be prepared. Do your homework

Remember the feather theory! Yes, you have a team supporting you. Use them and be confident. But do your homework. Remember you are wearing the most feathers. You better be able to wear them proudly and intelligently. Be prepared for many questions.

Know the history of the show you are directing. Be familiar with the playwright's canon of other works. If directing a period piece, know the period. If you are directing an absurdist drama, know what absurdism is.

Never go into any rehearsal without knowing what you want to accomplish. I've worked with many directors who work for the moment! I think that's just being lazy. Why are you directing the show? I would hope because you have a vision that you would like to share with others. Make sure you come prepared to the first rehearsal and every rehearsal that follows, ready to share that vision.

And be ready for any question. If you don't have the answer, be honest in your response, and then come to the next rehearsal with the answer.

An audition is not a polished performance

An audition is an opportunity to gauge a person's talent. It is not a time to see if an actor can play the part to perfection. Look for the qualities of the character in what an actor is auditioning with. Remember, you have weeks of rehearsal to develop the character.

I am always afraid of an actor who has the character down perfectly at an audition. Will they be able to take direction and develop into the character you want them to be?

At an audition for *Dames at Sea*, a redheaded woman sang a gutsy, belt song and she tap-danced up a storm. I thought she was perfect for the diva, Mona. I cast her on the spot. When we began rehearsal, she had a very difficult time learning the songs and the choreography. She couldn't memorize lines either. It turned out the only thing she could do was the song and dance she auditioned with. I eventually had to replace her in the role. What I should have done was asked her do some things at the audition to see if she could follow direction.

An audition should be a display of talent. Can the actor do the things you ask them to do? If they can, then they will be able to support your concept.

That's not to say that physical types don't exist. They do. But make sure they can do what you ask of them too.

Realism and the young

Students and beginning directors are so rooted in realism because they know film and television more than legitimate theatre, and that trend is affecting what they do in the real world of theatre. They don't understand anything that is not realism.

I can remember when I first began directing I thought everything had to be real. Real sets. Real props.

Theatre is not film. It can work with minimal sets. The Greeks did it and so did Shakespeare.

Each summer for eight years I worked with a program called MT Stage (Music Theatre Stage) through the Gifted Programs at University of Arkansas at Little Rock, and we wrote and produced shows without any sets or costumes very successfully.

All the actors wore a white T-shirt that was made for the program (the logo of the program was on the front of it), blue jeans, and tennis shoes. Costume pieces like a boa, sweater, hat, or tie were added to help establish character. The sets consisted of chairs, small tables, benches, or other small pieces. The locale was established in the dialogue like Shakespeare did. In one of the plays we needed a prison cell, so I put four backpacks on the stage floor to set the boundaries of the cell.

This will work in the theatre. It won't in film because film is so real. Stop thinking that you have to compete with the realism of film when doing a play.

You can keep it simple.

Simple vs. Spectacle

With the popularity of TV and film, many American directors have forgotten how simple theatre can be, especially with the way technology and the age of computers have changed everything. These directors have taken Aristotle's final component in his six key elements too far. Spectacle does not mean bombs going off.

Simply put, all Aristotle meant by "spectacle" was just the visual elements of the show. Sets, costumes, and lights. Each show has its own spectacle.

Waiting For Godot has a simple set, but that set is the "spectacle" of that show. Along with the costumes and the lights.

I served as the faculty advisory to some student-directed one-act plays. One of the directors insisted on having real western guns for the play he was directing. The purchase or even the rental of the guns was well out of our budget. He also wanted a set that was not possible financially. I tried to explain to him that simple is sometimes better than spectacle, especially with the farcical show he was directing.

He never understood what I was trying teach. He managed to get some real guns, and those guns did nothing but upstage the simple message of the show. The audience missed the point of the show because they were so focused on the real guns. A toy gun would have helped the show much more.

An audience will accept anything you throw at them. You don't need to hide the truth of a play with props, scenery, or costumes. The play's the thing! We cannot compete with Hollywood. Believe in convention.

Convention

Some theatre scholars have added convention to Aristotle's Six Key Elements as the seventh element. Convention is something you accept as a rule. Audiences willingly suspend their disbelief to accept a convention. When the lights fade on a scene, that means the scene is over or the show is over. If a character says that he is in a jail cell that is defined by four backpacks, the audience will accept that.

In my MFA playwriting thesis play *The Clown, The Penguin, and The Princess* at UNLV, there were characters flying throughout the entire show, just like in *Peter Pan*. When I wrote the play, I envisioned having the Las Vegas company Flying by Foy handle the flying element for the show. That didn't happen.

The convention that was used to establish when characters were flying work just as well as if Foy had actually flown them. Each character stood on a set piece, they held their arms out as though they were a plane flying, a green colored light hit them from the chest up, and as Stravinsky music played, the audience believed they were flying.

Once you establish a convention in a show, an audience will accept your offering as truth. There is no need to spend big bucks to be successful at good theatre.

Now, don't get me wrong. I love big spectacle, especially in musicals where part of the magic is the visual elements supporting the show. The moment in *Peter Pan* when Peter, Wendy, John, and Michael start to fly to Neverland, and the bedroom set breaks away and the walls, the beds, all disappears, leaving a background of a star filled night sky is probably my favorite moment of spectacle in all the shows I've directed.

Buts are beautiful

The word "but" in a line of dialogue is like a capital city being represented with a big star on a road map. Or better yet, a detour sign. Take heed! I can guarantee you that the playwright is giving you the other side of the issue, the statement with that "but." And the character probably believes more in the statement they say after the "but."

"I love you, Mom, but I know you killed dad!"

Don't speed through the "but." Treat it like a speed bump and slow down. And then have the actor change pitch on the second part of the statement.

Living in the conservative South

Doing shows can sometimes be difficult when living in the South. When I was teaching at a university in Arkansas, I wrote and directed a children's show, *The Tree Princess*. Broadway producers would kill for the kind of publicity and exposure this show received from the first read through to opening night.

I did a "no-no" in any play, especially a children's play, by killing off the title character. Other professors in the department were so worried that the play was going to warp the minds of the young audiences attending the show that a hold was put on opening night.

The script was given to the College of Education Professors to read to see if we were going to cause multitudes of children to go crazy by seeing a play where the title character dies.

We got a green light from the education people about the death. But how ironic it was that a bigger stink came because the show detailed a mother giving birth to a baby and the villain in the piece said "shut up" several times.

It's not just the South

I was directing a production of *Same Time, Next Year* at a college in central Minnesota. In the third scene, the female character walks in and says, "Hi, wanna fuck?" The chair of the department said I would have to cut that word.

I tried to explain that the scene was set in the sixties and the character was saying that word to get a specific reaction. She normally didn't talk that way and to say any other word would destroy the playwright's purpose.

We kept the word in and didn't get one complaint from the audiences. The bigger objection was that the two characters in the show were married people having an affair. So it's just not the South. And you never know what an audience is going to object to.

The lesson to be learned from these two stories is: Be bold and do what you feel is right.

Let it happen twice before you panic

When running scenes or acts and something an actor does is not what they've been doing at previous rehearsals, or not what you think they should be doing, don't panic. If it happens again at the next rehearsal, then panic.

Actually, all you have to do is talk to the actor about it. Get on the same page with him or her.

At a dress rehearsal, the young actress playing Liesl in *The Sound of Music* jumped in the air in jubilation after kissing Rolf, and in doing so she flashed her panties. Several people viewing the show told her about this, and the next night at rehearsal, her jump didn't have the height or verve that she'd been doing. I didn't think anything of it, but after it happened a second time, I spoke to her about what was wrong.

She said she didn't want to flash the audience again.

I told her about my "two times" theory.

She jumped with the needed verve the next night and through the rest of the run, and not once did her panties show again.

Use "in-one" scenes for what they were intended

Do you know what an "in-one" scene is? On a proscenium stage, think of the area in front of the proscenium arch/grand drape to the edge of the stage as the first position or the number one position. The second position would be from the grand drape to the first set of legs. So an "in-one" scene is a scene that is written to be played in front of the grand drape or show curtain (in the number one position). Its purpose is to allow the time for the set to be changed behind the curtain.

Show curtain for *Fiddler on the Roof* (Bock, Harnic, Stein)

This is usually used in musicals. Rodgers and Hammerstein employed this technique in many of their shows. In *The Sound of Music*, scene eight takes place in a hallway in the Von Trapp villa. The Von Trapp girls are walking in the hallway after singing "The Lonely Goatherd" in Maria's bedroom (scene seven). The only reason this hallway scene is in the show is to cover the

In the hall: *The Sound of Music* (Rodgers and Hammerstein)

time it takes the set to move from Maria's bedroom (scene seven) to the terrace of the Von Trapp villa (scene nine). The hallway scene should be played in front of the curtain without any set, so when the scene shift is completed, the show can move right on.

Too many productions treat "in-one" scenes as full scenes with sets, and it just slows the show down as the set is shifted to reflect a scene that was written not to have any scenery at all.

I've also incorporated this technique in nonmusicals. If a big scene shift is going to take place, I move the actors down stage (in the first position), lower the grand drape or just dim the lights upstage, shift the set as the scene is taking place, raise the curtain or bring the lights back up when the scene shift has been completed, and move right into the next scene without stopping the show or losing any time for a scene shift.

Two and a half hours

Speaking of Rodgers and Hammerstein musicals. The first act in all their musicals is always an hour and a half, and the second act is an hour. If your R and H musical is lasting any longer than that, you're not utilizing the in-one scenes, or your tempo is just too slow.

The producer and director relationship

Remember my feather theory? The producer has the most feathers. He's the chief of the theatre tribe. He is the Big Kahuna. He signs the checks and ultimately has the final say in everything.

But (here's a "beautiful but") a smart producer trusts the director that he has hired. They let the director do his or her job. Unfortunately, there are some producers who don't let a director do their job; they try to do it for them.

It's like in sports where the owner of a professional team doesn't let the coach or manager do the job they were hired to do. Some owners interfere too much. George Steinbrenner of the Yankees or Jerry Jones of the Cowboys come to mind.

A producer does have the right to dictate things to the director, but if it gets excessive, the show will suffer. These differences should have been worked out before rehearsal began.

Early in my career, I worked with a producer who would come in to a rehearsal after a scene was blocked and then make changes to the blocking. Not just minor changes, he would damn near restage the entire scene.

I have always prided myself on my blocking and have been complimented on how well I staged shows. I thought maybe he knew something I didn't and could learn from him, but when he started using my blocking in one scene that was cut from another, I knew he was just pulling a power play.

I didn't understand why he was even paying me to direct. It was obvious he wanted to direct the show. I finally figured out that he couldn't be at all the rehearsals, and I was being paid to make sure the actors were doing what he wanted them to do. I was just a stage manager.

If this happens while you're directing, I would step down and let the producer direct the show.

Yelling at actors

Directing can be very frustrating. And everything that is going wrong with a show ultimately gets blamed on you, the director. That doesn't give you the right to treat the actors like dogs who just pooped on the floor. Actually, you shouldn't even treat a dog like what I'm talking about.

Yelling at actors doesn't accomplish anything positive. It just makes the actors think of you as a bully, and they stop trying to please. Thus the show suffers.

If you want to raise your voice, do it with enthusiasm—it's much more rewarding.

Make a sign that says "smile"

Characters in musicals should be smiling when they are singing. All right, Sweeny Todd doesn't smile much. I'm really talking about characters in the chorus of big musical comedies. They smile as they sing. And smiling means open your eyes wide and smile with teeth showing.

I used to say "smile" so much during rehearsals for musicals and in notes after rehearsal that I finally just made a sign out of cardboard that read, "SMILE," in BIG BLOCK LETTERS! During each musical number the stage manager, assistant stage manager, or I would walk through the audience holding the sign high above our heads.

I've also been known to hang that sign in the control booth window at the back of the theatre during performances.

I've never met an actor who is bad on purpose

I've directed over four hundred and fifty shows and have seen thousands, and in all those shows I've seen some bad actors. But in all those shows, I've never seen an actor who was acting badly on purpose. Yes, there have been actors who were mad about contracts or something personal, and they didn't try as hard as they could, but I'm not talking about that.

Actors always give one hundred percent to their performances. The thing to remember is not all actors are at the same level in their craft. Some actors might be putting out one hundred percent, but they are just not as developed in their craft as others. Don't write them off as bad actors; they are just developing actors.

I know that doesn't help your show, but keep working with them. They want your coaching, and one day you'll see that it pays off.

Assistant Director or assistant to the Director

An assistant director is someone who helps direct the show. Not a codirector, but someone who has some artistic responsibility. An assistant to the director is there to do what the director wishes. From getting coffee to running a scene for lines. Some call the assistant to the director a gopher.

Callbacks

Over the years, I've decided that I don't need to have callbacks. I usually know who I want for each part, and callbacks were just a waste of time. If I do have a callback, it is usually only to see physical types.

However, callbacks do give you the opportunity to see an actor for a second time. Or to pair actors together to see how they look side by side.

Don't feel obligated to have callbacks just because it is standard procedure.

If an actor has a question about a costume

When an actor starts asking questions about the way a costume fits or its color, that usually means they have a problem with the costume, and they already have the answer to their question. Be careful how you answer, you don't want to anger the actor, they do have to perform.

Does this costume make me look fat? Obviously, it does to the actor. Do these shoes match the dress? To the actor, they don't. Would my character wear this style? The actor doesn't think so.

Many of these questions can be eliminated if at the first rehearsal the costume designer has shared the designs with the cast. But if questions still come up at the first dress, remind the actor that it is not them in the costume; it is the character. Another good thing to remind them (which is the truth) is to never judge a costume under the light in the dressing room. Wait to see what it looks like under stage lighting, next to the other costumes on stage.

Straight lines only look good in a Follies kick line

Straight lines don't belong on a stage. Remember, you're trying to tell a story through blocking and composition. A straight line flattens a stage picture, gives it no depth, and doesn't tell story, unless you're doing *A Chorus Line*, and then the straight line is telling story.

Spoofing *A Chorus Line* with straight line: *Joseph and the Amazing Technicolor Dreamcoat* (Lloyd-Webber and Rice)

Don't forget the triangle theory, the use of levels, and body positions.

The last tip

When a show is good, the critics and audiences always seem to credit the performers, but when a show is bad, the blame is put on the director. When you are hot, you're every actor's best friend, and when you're going through an off period, actors don't even look your way.

Being the boss in a collaborative art can sometimes feel very lonely, but being prepared and sure of your vision, treating all collaborators as equals, and having good material, will earn you the respect the position calls for.

Final Thoughts

These theories/practices didn't come to me overnight or as I directed my first show. I had been developing them since before that first show and with all the hundreds that followed. I borrowed from mentors, books, and other directors, and developed my own process. They have proven themselves, stood the test of time, and helped me earn the 17.3 million I earn annually.

My techniques will give you a solid foundation. Use them all or just some. Add these theories to your existing directing knowledge and make them your own. The process of directing is an ever-changing craft and an ongoing learning experience with each show you bring to life.

Break a leg.

SPECIAL THANKS

As I said at the beginning of the book, there are five individuals who deserve special thanks for their influence on my directing career. I'd like to pay homage to these important collaborators here with a short tribute to each.

Dick Cermele as Tevye in *Fiddler on the Roof* (Bock, Harnick, and Stein)

Dick Cermele, my directing mentor in undergraduate school at St. Cloud State University (MN), opened my eyes to what the art of directing was really all about. It was all through dissecting a script so that I knew every breath the script took. It's all about units and beats. And objectives. Years after I graduated, I had the honor of directing a production of *Fiddler on the Roof* with him playing Tevye.

Kari Anderson on the set of *The Fantasticks* (Jones and Schmidt)

Kari Anderson and I were young when we began to work together (1980). She was a choreographer with the same passion for dance as I had for the directing, and she brought life to musical numbers with the same verve I did with the book scenes. We complimented each other like twins.

We did eleven musicals together in the 1980s in Minneapolis, MN, before we both moved to different parts of the county. We reunited in 2013 to do a production of *The Fantasticks* back in Minneapolis. The magic was still there.

Joy Breckenridge was a costume designer who could capture the essence of each character on stage with the clothing she put them in. A character didn't have to speak, and the audience knew who they were by what they were wearing. She helped me understand characters more through her designs. Joy was the costume designer at St. Cloud State University in the early 70s when I was a student there. We reunited in 1994 when we both taught at the University of Arkansas at Little Rock. She designed costumes and I directed.

Joy Breckenridge

Lynn Musgrave, Minneapolis' gift to acting, taught me that men and women characters don't react identically in the same situation. She played God in Arthur Miller's *The Creation of the World and Other Business* the second time I directed that show (1984). The first time I did it, a male played God. Toward the climax of the play, there comes a moment when God is very sad at what has happened with Adam and Eve. The first time I did the show, I told the actor playing God not to cry when showing his emotion, to fight the tears, it would be stronger.

Lynn Musgrave as God in *The Creation of the World and Other Business* (Miller)

I told Lynn the same thing when we got to that moment in the production she played God. If she cried, it would show that God was weak. She pointed out that women don't hide their emotions like men do. She cried, the scene worked wonderfully, and I began to look at characters' emotions through feelings other than my male ways.

My teachings live on through Cris Tibbetts, a former student of mine, an actor, a playwriting collaborator with me, and a friend turned fine director. We first met each other in 1987.

He was the original Beanie in *Beanie and the Bamboozling Book Machine* in 1989. Twenty years later, he revived that same character in the fourth sequel to *Beanie* titled *The Wizard of Bamboozlement* (2009).

Cris Tibbetts as Beanie in *The Wizard of Bamboozlement* (May)

We continue to keep on top of the directing art through our critiques of each other's work.

About the Author

Bob May began his theatre career as an actor in 1967 doing a small role in *Kiss Me Kate* at Ft. Lauderdale (FL) High School. After acting in many stage productions in Southern Florida and doing various print and commercial work, including *Seventeen Magazine*, Polaroid Cameras, Polaroid Sunglasses, and Columbia Record Club he moved to Southern California to give Hollywood a try. A call back for *The Dating Game* was never attended as he chased his heart to Minnesota.

Acting took a backseat to directing while he earned a BA in theatre from St. Cloud (MN) State University in 1972. Since that time he has directed over 450 productions at various educational, community, and professional theatres across the country; winning numerous awards for his directing.

Of course while directing all those shows, he was teaching acting and coaching actors. Bob began teaching in higher education in 1983 and has taught acting and directing at Brainerd (MN) Community College, the University of Nevada Las Vegas, the University of Arkansas at Little Rock, the University of Central Arkansas, and Mountview Theatre School in London, England.

As he was teaching, he was also writing plays and to date over fifty of his plays have been produced and twenty-three have been published. At Brainerd Community College his plays *Paul Bunyan - Lumberjack Extraordinaire, The Three Little Pigs, Beanie and the Bamboozling Book Machine* (published by Samuel French) and *The Andrew is Dead Story* (an AIDS play, published by I. E. Clark) were produced.

In 1994 Bob earned an MFA in playwriting from the University of Nevada, Las Vegas. During his tenure at UNLV, the university theatre produced eight of his plays, including *Faces, For the Love of a Woman, Concerned Citizen* (published by Dramatic Publishing), and *The Clown, The Penguin, and The Princess*.

His plays *Broadway Memories* and *9th Inning Wedding* are published in the textbook, *The Golden Stage* by Ann McDonough, Ph.D.

Bob currently teaches Playwriting and Screenwriting at the University of Central Arkansas. Since moving to Arkansas, he has written two sequels to his popular play *Beanie and the Bamboozling Book Machine*. They are *Beanie and the Bamboozling Horror Machine* and *Beanie and the Bamboozling Adventure Machine* (both published by Samuel French).

He served as Artistic Director and wrote all the plays that his Children's Theatre to Go theatre company produced in its eight-year history. They include *Crystal and the Christmas Snowman, A Different Kind of Nutcracker*, and *Elson - the First Christmas Elf* (all published in the collection: *Snowmen, Elves, and Nutcrackers* by Baker Plays), *Cinderella and the Fairy Godfather, Alice in Wonderland, Gidget's Gadget to Bamboozle Beanie, Hocus Pocus Horticulture*, and *Snow White and the Magic Mirror* (all published by Playscripts Inc.), and *Jack and Bella: From Beanstalk to Broadway*, a musical of the Jack and the Beanstalk tale (published by Heuer Publishing). Brooklyn Publishers published *The Great Santa Claus Reindeer Roundup*.

His absurdist play *Go To...* is published in the 2009 literary journal *The Exquisite Corpse* and by Heuer Publishing.

He wrote The Gulf Coastal Plains Region episode for the Arkansas Educational Television Network (PBS) program *The Great Experience of Arkansas: An Amazing Journey Through Six Regions*.

He and his wife, Cathy, have a blended family of five children and six grandchildren. Bob is a member of The Dramatists Guild of America.

Other Theatre Books by Bob May

Postcard Pointers to the Performer
(Dominion Publications)
Scriptwriting Structure: To-the-Point Pointers
(Skye Bridge Publishing)

Show Credits

All productions directed by Bob May (except *City Lights* and *Under the Gaslight*).

Beanie and the Bamboozling Book Machine - University of Central Arkansas, Conway, Arkansas. Set Designer: April Allen. Costume Designer: Annaliese Baker. Photo by Gregory Blakey

Chicago – Centre Stage, Minneapolis, Minnesota. Set Designer: Bob Platte. Costume Designer: Dwight Larson. Choreographer: Kari Anderson. Photo by Jacqueline Henning.

City Lights – Flamingo-Hilton, Las Vegas, Nevada.

Company – Theatre 1900, Minneapolis, Minnesota. Choreographer: Kari Anderson. Set and Costume Designer: Dwight Larson. Photo by Jacqueline Henning.

Creation of the World and Other Business, The (First Production) – The Prairie Stage, Waverly, Minnesota. Set and Costume Designer and photo by Jacqueline Henning.

Creation of the World and Other Business, The (Second Production) – Centre Stage, Minneapolis, Minnesota. Set Designer: Max Green. Costume Designer: Dwight Larson. Photo by Jacqueline Henning.

Elson: The First Christmas Elf – Children's Theatre To Go, Conway, Arkansas. Costume Designer: Nikki Webster. Set Designer: Joe Meils. Photo by Teresa Scheuter.

The Fantasticks – Theatre in the Round, Minneapolis, Minnesota. Set Designer: Sadie Ward, Costume Designer: Dwight Larson. Lighting Designer: Daniel Ellis. Choreographer: Kari Anderson.

Fiddler on the Roof – Centre Stage, Minneapolis, Minnesota. Set Designer: Bob Platte. Costume Designer: Dwight Larson. Photo by Jacqueline Henning.

Flea in Her Ear, A - Elk River Community Theatre, Elk River, Minnesota. Costume Designer: Peta Barrett. Set Designer and photo by Jacqueline Henning.

Great Santa Claus Reindeer Roundup, The – Prompt Book by Bob May, Children's Theatre to Go, Conway, Arkansas.
Hocus Pocus Horticulture – Children's Theatre to Go, Conway, Arkansas. Set Designer: Joe Meils. Costume Designer: Nikki Webster. Photo by Teresa Scheuter.
Jack and Bella: From Beanstalk to Broadway – Children's Theatre to Go, Conway, Arkansas. Costume Designer: Nikki Webster. Set Designer: Joe Meils. Photo by Teresa Scheuter.
Joseph and the Amazing Technicolor Dreamcoat - Centre Stage, Minneapolis, Minnesota. Set Designer: Jim Erdahl. Costume Designer: Peta Barrett. Photo by Jacqueline Henning.
Lion in Winter, The – The Prairie Stage, Waverly, Minnesota. Set Designer: Jacqueline Henning. Costume Designer: Christine Exley. Photo by Jacqueline Henning.
Not Enough Rope – Prompt book by Bob May, St. Cloud State University, St. Cloud, Minnesota.
Pippin – Centre Stage, Minneapolis, Minnesota. Set and Costume Designer: Dwight Larson. Photo by Jacqueline Henning.
Quilters – Brainerd Community College Theatre. Set and Costume Designer: Dennis Lamberson.
Run for Your Wife – Floor Plan by Dennis Lamberson - Brainerd Community College Theatre, Brainerd, Minnesota.
Shot in the Dark, A – Rochester Civic Theatre, Rochester, Minnesota. Set Designer: Gary Schattschneider.
Sound of Music, The – Brainerd Community College, Brainerd, Minnesota. Set and Costume Designer: Dennis Lamberson.
Trixie True Teen Detective – Entrance/exit graph by Bob May - Theatre 1900, Minneapolis, MN.
Under the Gaslight – Bob May as Byke - University of Nevada, Las Vegas.
West Side Story – Minnetonka Theatre, Minnetonka, Minnesota. Set Designer: Bob Platte. Costume Designer: Peta Barrett. Photo by Jacqueline Henning.
Wizard of Bamboozlement, The – Children's Theatre to Go, Conway, Arkansas. Set Designer: Joe Meils. Costume Designer: Nikki Webster. Photo by Teresa Scheuter.

Working – Centre Stage, Minneapolis, Minnesota. Set Designer: Jim Erdahl. Costume Designer: Peta Barrett. Photo by Jacqueline Henning.

List of Authors Whose Plays Appear in Photographs and Figures

Achard, Marcel
Bernstein, Leonard
Bock, Jerry
Booth, Roy C.
Bradford, Chad
Cooney, Ray
Damashak, Barbara
Ebb, Fred
Feydeau, Georges
Furth, George
Goldman, James
Hammerstein, Oscar
Hamilton, Kelly
Harnick, Sheldon
Hirson, Roger
Jensen, Mark
Jones, Tom

Kander, John
Laurents, Arthur
Lloyd-Webber, Andrew
May, Bob
May, Elaine
Miller, Arthur
Newman, Molly
Owings, Karen
Rice, Tim
Rodgers, Richard
Jerome Robbins
Schmidt, Harvey
Schwartz, Stephen
Sondheim, Stephen
Stein, Joseph
Tibbetts, Cris

Notes

Notes

www.ingramcontent.com/pod-product-compliance
Lightning Source LLC
Chambersburg PA
CBHW050542300426
44113CB00012B/2219